THE TIME TRIAL

Jack Gilhooley

BROADWAY PLAY PUBLISHING INC
224 E 62nd St, NY, NY 10065
www.broadwayplaypub.com
info@broadwayplaypub.com

THE TIME TRIAL
© Copyright 2014 by Jack Gilhooley

First printing: December 2014
I S B N: 978-0-88145-612-7

Book design: Marie Donovan
Page make-up: Adobe Indesign
Typeface: Palatino
Printed and bound in the U S A

THE TIME TRIAL had a 24-performance workshop
production by the New York Shakespeare Festival
(Joseph Papp, Producer; Bernard Gersten, Associate
Producer) at the Public Theatre, opening on 29 April
1975. The cast and creative contributors were:

SLIME .... Tracey Walter
CANDY .... Diane Stilwell
ZIGGIE .... Tom Lee Jones
GLENNA RAE .... Ellen Sandler
BO PEEP .... Jayne Haynes
RICKY .... Robert Burgos
SLICK .... Graham Beckel

Director .... Peter Maloney
Setting .... John Pitt
Costumes .... Patricia McGourty
Lighting .... Spencer Mosse
Music .... David Maloney
Lyrics .... Jack Gilhooley

The play was published by Broadway Play Publishing
Inc in September 1986 in *Plays From The New York
Shakespeare Festival.*

THE TIME TRIAL was subsequently produced by
Steep Theatre Company in Chicago, running from 27
May 27 through 26 June 2004. The cast and creative
contributor were:

SLIME .... Peter Moore
CANDY .... Liz Wharton
ZIGGIE .... Alex Gillmor
GLENNA RAE .... Kelli Cousins
BO PEEP .... Sadie Rogers
RICKY .... Michael Rice
SLICK .... Anderson Lawfer

Director .... Lauren Golanty

In 2008 the author did a considerable update and
overhaul to reflect contemporary America.

CHARACTERS

all in their 20s

CARLTON "TOAD" PINE, *a slovenly whipping boy. Smallish and perhaps mildly retarded.* ZIGGY's *"fool", he's savvy enough to know that he's the butt of jokes but he knows he's got a place here. And that's precious to him.*

CANDY, *a sweet and pretty blonde young woman trying to be bad.*

ZIGGIE, *mean, handsome (or better yet, handsome/ugly). Head honcho (for now).*

GLENNA RAE, *pretty but dissipated. Too smart to be here but she's trapped.*

BO PEEP, *a local mixed-race singer at roadhouses on weekends. Given her moderate musical talent, she's the one with the best chance of escape.*

RICKY RUANE, *disabled Iraq War vet. Walks with a limp. Angry (of course).*

SLICK, *strong, silent Tiresias of the group. Former H S football star with* ZIGGIE. *Wears overalls. African-American.*

An offstage announcer's voice (can be M or F ie Casey/ Cassie?)

SETTING

Time: First decade of the 21st century
Place: Small town America

ACT ONE—*A tiny corner of an auto raceway grandstand in the morning.*

ACT TWO—*An automobile graveyard at night (the early A M following ACT ONE)*

Music strongly suggested but please avoid the cliché *of country & western.*

THE TIME TRIAL is not intended as a strictly naturalistic play. Rather, the director/designer team should conceptualize "off-center realism". How far off is a matter of choice but the automobile graveyard definitely *needn't* have a *real* car onstage. Ideally, something resembling a Chamberlain auto-collage with the brightly painted number five on the hood.

Nor need the wreck be composed of real auto parts especially since the car has been smashed beyond recognition. A designer who works in light sheet metal—or a variation—might conceivably be able to create the effect.

Other suggestions: the shell of a junked car could be transported onstage. The designer could paint the 5 on the hood and then the crew could sledgehammer it. Or perhaps only the hood area could jut out from the wings.

This is all meant to convince a producing company that they don't have to transport a car onstage.

Rather than documentary realism, the staging could lean towards choreography at times. When for instance, a crash seems imminent the actors should "rivet", not to the point of a stylized freeze but enough so that there should be a sense of suspended animation. With the possibility of a physical confrontation the actors should "scramble" to vantage points.

Finally, despite the summer's oppressive heat, these seven outcasts are rambunctious and troublesome post-delinquents. They practice their marginal criminality with pride and camaraderie in a languid environment.

ACT ONE

(The play opens on the far corner of the "Speed" Larsen Speedway.)

(The characters will sit—or romp—on raked stands. A two or three-tiered bleacher would work [or plain seatless levels]. Perhaps *a faux concrete wall—with product logos—separates the actors from the audience.)*

(At rise, a young man with a battered face. He watches an approaching race car and his head pivots as it zooms past.We should have the notion that Carlton ["Toad"] is a bit "off". He may be slack-jawed or his eyes could droop on occasion. His clothes are raggedy with pants held up by an overlong belt His shirt is long-sleeved.)

(TOAD touches his wounded face and winces.)

PUBLIC ADDRESS: *(Off)* And that was Sutter Sinclair of Tuscaloosa, Alabama.driving his '97 Bobcat Superstreak.

TOAD: ATTA GO, SUTTER!!! THE PEDAL T' THE METAL. *(As he sits he gestures and utters quiet instructions)* Only don't cut that turn so wide. *(After a blank stare, he spies a trash can. He crosses and starts tossing stuff from the can until he finds a crumpled sheet of tin foil. He takes a ball of foil from his pocket and attaches the new-found material, packing it down with pride.)*

(ZIGGIE—*carrying binoculars*—*and* CANDY *enter from the rear and can't see* TOAD'*s face.* CANDY *only cares about auto racing because* ZIGGIE *does.*)

CANDY: Hiya, Toad.

ZIGGIE: Whatcha got there, boy?

(TOAD *turns toward them, extending proudly his ball of foil.* CANDY *and* ZIGGIE *see his bruises for the first time.*)

CANDY: Jeez-usssss. What the hell happened to you?

TOAD: *(Smile…shrug)* Life.

CANDY: Life???

TOAD: *(Proudly)* Fight club!

(ZIGGIE *just shakes his head in despair as* CANDY *crosses, concerned.*)

CANDY: Toad, ya can't keep doin' this. You're gonna get yerself killed.

TOAD: I can handle myself.

ZIGGIE: I'm not aware of any fight club hereabouts. Where the fuck d'you go, boy?

TOAD: *(Mantra-like)* The first rule of fight club is, you don't talk about fight club.

CANDY: You drive down to the city last night?

TOAD: The first rule of fight club is—

ZIGGIE: I hope you're packin' I D so they know where to ship the body. *(Scruffing his neck affectionately)* You gotta wash that mug a'yours. Cleanliness is next t'godliness. You never heard that?

(TOAD *shakes his head.*)

CANDY: That's cause you're growin' potatoes in yer ears.

TOAD: *(Tucking his shirt in, sort of)* Actually yeah, I heard it. I just never believed it.

ZIGGIE: You got somethin' for Toad's face, Nurse Candy?

TOAD: *(Smirking)* Hah! *Nurse* Candy.

CANDY: How 'bout a bag?

ZIGGIE: You get any money for that fight club whuppin'?

TOAD: No, but some of those boys go on T V. Mixed Martial Arts. That's where the money is. *(He strikes his martial arts stance…badly.)*

ZIGGIE: They don't put punchin' bags on T V.

TOAD: Sure they do. Somebody gotta lost. An' I'm still learnin' the sport.

CANDY: Learnin' was never your strong point.

(TOAD re-deposits the trash. CANDY stares off.)

CANDY: Not a sign of 'em. Hey Toad, you seen a sign of 'em?

(TOAD shakes his head.)

CANDY: We shouldn'a listened to dizzy-ass Glenna Rae. Zig, you better check the stash when they get here. They're prob'ly off getting' stoned and laughin' up their sleeve at us.

(TOAD raises his sleeve and mock-laughs ["Ha-ha-ha"]. CANDY glares as he amusedly retreats.)

CANDY: We oughtta go lookin' for those assholes.

ZIGGIE: They'll come to us, Candy. Just sit back an' wait for the next run.

TOAD: Hey Zig, maybe she's right. I wouldn't trust Glenna an' those otha mothas.

ZIGGIE: None of 'em has the guts to cop what's mine. Beside, Glenna won't miss ole Speed.

CANDY: Yeah, she won't pass up the chance to see Speed in his time trial .

Say, why do they need to race the clock? Why not just let 'em all cut loose tomorra?

ZIGGIE: You don't much care for this sport, huh Candy?

CANDY: *(Shrugs)* Driver drivin' around the track 'til some guy waves a tablecloth. That's a sport?

TOAD: That's it! You just hit it, babe.

CANDY: Don't you call me "babe".

TOAD: You're a babe. What's wrong with that?

CANDY: You're sayin' it is what's wrong. Only Ziggie calls me "Babe".

ZIGGIE: It's O K, Candy. I don't have it copyrighted.

CANDY: Well…maybe you should.

P A *(Off)* An' Sutter Sinclair qualifies.

TOAD: See, a time trial is a qualifyin' heat.

CANDY: Well, why does Speed-o Larsen have to qualify? They named the fuckin' track after him. Doesn't that qualify him?

TOAD: Everybody gotta qualify.

CANDY: Car ever go outta control in a time trial?

TOAD: Nah. Hardly never.

CANDY: I'm goin' home, then. Catch me some shut-eye.

ZIGGIE: But a car could overheat…catch fire…blow the driver to smithereens.

CANDY: *(Reflecting)* Well, maybe I'll just stick around, then. *(Sitting)*

TOAD: But crashes are more likely durin' the race tomorrow.

CANDY: Well then, maybe I'll just catch a snooze in yer truck, Zig.

(As CANDY's *leaving,* TOAD *and* ZIGGIE *quasi-surreptitiously tease.)*

ZIGGIE: Good riddance t'her, huh Toad?

TOAD: *(Grinning)* Don't know why they let girls in the raceway, anyways.

ZIGGIE: Who'd fetch our beer?

(They're playful good-ole-boys-in-training. ZIGGIE *puts his arm around* TOAD *who revels in the camaraderie.)*

CANDY: *(Returning)* Changed my mind. I'll stay just to spite you guys. An' to keep you two from cuddlin' with each other.

(The boys laugh and whoop. TOAD *"cuddles" mock-girlishly with* ZIGGIE.*)*

ZIGGIE: You're a cold-hearted woman, Candy. Afflicted with bloodlust.

CANDY: Of all things to call me. Cold hearted? The things I do for you...

TOAD: *(Cackling)* What things d'you do for Zig?

*(*TOAD's *crossed the line.* ZIGGIE *withdraws and stares at him.* TOAD *sobers in confusion and regret.)*

CANDY: Hey Zig, Glenna told me that Speed's the only guy she ever loved. The real deal. I mean y'know... "love", loved. Y'know?

ZIGGIE: Do I know? Do I know "love", loved?

*(*CANDY *nods in anticipation.)*

ZIGGIE: Well no I don't, Candy. That's goin' a bit overboard to my thinkin'. Love alone, seems a perfectly good emotion. You shouldn't be greedy. It can turn on you. Bite yer ass.

(CANDY nods dutifully.)

TOAD: Speed's just the first guy she ever boned. First in a long parade.

CANDY: You'll never march in that parade, Toad-man.

TOAD: I wouldn't touch 'er unless a doctor checked 'er out.

CANDY: You'd do more'n touch 'er 'cept she won't get near your cage.

TOAD: *(Quietly thoughtless)* I get mine, Candy.

(CANDY and ZIGGIE react simultaneously and angrily. ZIGGIE springs at terrified TOAD.)

CANDY: YOU SCUMMY LITTLE DIRT BAG!!!

ZIGGIE: *(Overlapping)*	TOAD: *(Grabbing him)*
You better watch how you talk about my woman! *(Grabbing him)* You're nothin' more'n a lump a'shit. Go out t'the truck an fetch that jug a'wine.	I'm sorry... It slipped out... Honest, Zig. Don't hurt me. I am that, Zig. It'll never happen again.

(Released, TOAD heads off obediently.)

ZIGGIE: IT HAPPENED ONCE AND ONCE ONLY!

CANDY: AN' DON'T YOU EVER TELL ANYONE!

TOAD: *(Index finger to his lips)* Lips're sealed.

ZIGGIE: You rat out Candy an' they'll be sealed in cement. Now get a move on.

(ZIGGIE kicks at TOAD who scampers off. Long pause. ZIGGIE crosses to dejected CANDY.)

CANDY: When did that little turdball ever hurry anywhere?

(Whimpering)

ZIGGIE: You heard me. It ain't gonna happen again.

CANDY: Once is more than enough.

ZIGGIE: Hey, it ain't like you had *real* sex with him. We were all doped up…drunk an' such. Nobody's responsible. Besides, it was an act of mercy.

CANDY: No mercy for me!

ZIGGIE: You gave him a bath out at the quarry. Like a dog. That was all.

CANDY: Wasn't "all".

ZIGGIE: He's a health hazard. You got him a postponement. You're a regular Angel of Mercy.

CANDY: Bull. I didn't mind so much his back…his greasy hair, even. His moldy feet, even.

ZIGGIE: You made a man outta him.

CANDY: But nooooo, that wasn't enough for alla you guys.

ZIGGIE: Look, the boy got excited. Aroused. Had an accident of nature. Nothin' unnatural.

CANDY: Well, it sure ain't *natural* A quarry's not a bathtub an' I'm not one a'them dick-washin' Chinese geishas.

ZIGGIE: I see it as a compassionate civic duty.

CANDY: Yeah, well folks weren't laughin' at compassion.

ZIGGIE: We laughed at Toad.

CANDY: Why didn't Bo Peep wash 'im? Why not Glenna Rae?

ZIGGIE: Because Candace, you are pretty beyond words. And they're a pair of skanks next t'you.

CANDY: Well, since you put it that way…

ZIGGIE: It's probably as close as he'll ever come to the real thing with a girl. So at least he'll live with a beautiful recollect—

CANDY: It ain't beautiful if I was disgusted.

ZIGGIE: It ain't about you alla time, Candy.

CANDY: Why don't we dump that runt?

ZIGGIE: 'Cause he's *our* runt. *(Diverting her)* Hey, hey, looka here.

(Faint motor sound. ZIGGIE uses the battered binoculars.)

CANDY: Is it Speed?

ZIGGIE: *(Shakes his head)* That punk-ass from the West Coast drivin' a Panther II.

(ZIGGIE offers CANDY the glasses. She declines.)

CANDY: Ya seen one, ya seen 'em all.

P A: *(Off)* From Fresno, California, drivin' a Panther II, Billy Harland...

ZIGGIE: What'd I tell ya?

CANDY: Must be a market for a mind like yours. *(Deflecting ZIGGIE's stare)* Only kiddin', Zig.

(The car roars off. CANDY and ZIGGIE follow its path.)

CANDY: Is Mister Billy Harland doin' good?

ZIGGIE: Can't touch Speed. He'll kick ass an' take numbers offa these diddleyshitters.

CANDY: Zig, how come if'n Speed's so good he comes back t'this second-rate track in this asswipe town? He usta race at Minneapolis...an' that big one in Europe.

ZIGGIE: Indianapolis! An' the Grand Prix.

CANDY: That's how you say it? Pree? P-R-I-Xx? Man, iff'n you say that like it's spelled... *(Giggles)* ...why, that's a whole other contest.

(CANDY *laughs heartily but* ZIGGIE *is unamused.*)

ZIGGIE: "Pree". It's French.

CANDY: So what, I'm not. *(Laughs)* 'Cept for kissin'. It's "pricks" t'me. *(She laughs alone then mimies a mike and plays the announcer.)* YES SIRREE, LADIES AND GENTS, THE WINNER OF THIS YEAR'S GRAND PRICKS, MISTER GORDON "ZIGGIE" HUTTON. UNANIMOUS...HANDS DOWN WINNER. HE GOT THE GRANDEST PRICK OF ALL!!! WHEEEEEEEEEEE-HOOOOO!!!

(ZIGGIE *is amused as usual with free-spirited* CANDY.)

ZIGGIE: It ain't a bad track. Best in the region. It's all this place is known for.

CANDY: That an' the state hog callin' contest.

ZIGGIE: Speed come back for us.

CANDY: "Us"? You 'n me?

ZIGGIE: His home folks. They named the track after him. So he came home to show gratitude.

CANDY: He's only grateful for havin' got out.

P A: *(Off)* An' Billy Harland is a qualifier. Atta boy, Billy.

ZIGGIE: Always a class dude. When my daddy got killed Hollis took me under his wing.

CANDY: "Hollis"?

ZIGGIE: He was born Hollis but he earned "Speed".

CANDY: I should think so...name like "Hollis".

ZIGGIE: He was like a big brother. He took me huntin'...fishin'. Once I hooked me a big ole channel cat. Pulled me right inta the drink. *(Smiling as he appreciatively reminisces)* I couldn't swim a lick. He just laughed as I thrashed aroun' preparin' t'meet The

Lord. But he scooped me out just as I was goin' under.
I was pissed. But I owed him my life.

CANDY: Sounds like a jerk t'me.

ZIGGIE: Next week I signed on for swimmin' lessons at
the Y.

CANDY: You're the best swimmer at the quarry.

ZIGGIE: I owe it all to Speed. I grew up an' he taught
me cars. Taught me more than any school.

CANDY: Ricky Roo says he's spooked…says Speed is
chickenshit now.

ZIGGIE: He *what*???

CANDY: I'm merely conveyin' Rick's point of view.

(TOAD *re-enters cautiously with a jug of wine.*)

TOAD: What'd I miss?

CANDY: *(Eager to change the subject)* Guy just qualified.

TOAD: No shit!

CANDY: Billy someone.

TOAD: No shit!

ZIGGIE: Where'd you hear Ricky Roo talk that kinda
trash?

CANDY: Well…we was up at Provosnik's Paradise on
379 droppin' reds an' drinkin' "Rocks". Ricky started
talkin' about Speed an' how he was the only one
who made it big outta here. An' I says, "How about
Marsha Enright on *Return To The Edge of Dawn*"? An'
bigmouth Bo says, "She usta wear the biggest braces in
town. Look like the grill of a Rolls Royce." Everybody
laughed. Then I said, "Marsha's a dyke. Everyone
knows that."

TOAD: I didn't.

CANDY: Well, everyone who's not sleepwalkin'. Then Bo says, "I hated Marsha En—"

ZIGGIE: FUCK MARSHA ENRIGHT!!!

CANDY: Not likely, Zig. She's a dyke.

ZIGGIE: TELL ME ABOUT RICKY!!!

TOAD: Here's your wine, Zig. I forgot t'pee. *(He starts off.)*

ZIGGIE: Get back here.

(TOAD returns reluctantly and rivets on the track.)

CANDY: Realize, Rick was flyin' high an' he's still got that P T S D from Eye-raq. He just come out an' says… You tell 'im, Toad.

TOAD: I dunno nothin'.

CANDY: Ain't that the truth. But you can hear an' iff'n'—

ZIGGIE: If one or the other of you morons don't—

CANDY: O K, O K…Rick said Speed's been spooked ever since he crashed. No heart no more.

TOAD: No balls since Daytona.

ZIGGIE: Ricky said that about Speed?

TOAD: Said his days are numbered.

CANDY: Said Speed'll be doin' hot rods soon.

TOAD: "Funny cars"…

CANDY: Be drag racin' the Mexicans on Highway 27.

ZIGGIE: Was Glenna there?

CANDY: Sorta. She was passed out on the shuffleboard.

P A: *(Off)* O K folks, here's L A Carpenter from Huntsville, Alabama drivin' his Lynx Alhambra I.

(TOAD has opened the bottle and is about to swig. ZIGGIE intercepts. The car zooms away.)

ZIGGIE: *(Grabbing the bottle)* Hey, what'd I tell you about that?

TOAD: It's like…tonic. I'm hurtin'.

CANDY: You gonna be sick, get away from me.

ZIGGIE: *(To TOAD)* Tough titty. But this ain't no community jug where you're concerned.

CANDY: You're unhygienic, Toad.

TOAD: I don't have a cup.

ZIGGIE: Well, getcher yerself one then you can drink t'your heart's content.

(TOAD heads for the trash can but CANDY and ZIGGIE stare disdainfully. He heads off.)

(ZIGGIE swigs and passes the jug to CANDY. She swigs awkwardly and grimaces.)

CANDY: L A Carpenter's doin' pretty good.

ZIGGIE: 'At boy's only some cracker drivin' a bucket of grease.

CANDY: Speed oughtta whip him, huh?

ZIGGIE: When we were just little squirts we'd climb over that fence *(Thumbing off)* t'watch Speed startin' out.

CANDY: Not me. I wasn't raised up here, remember? So I can't get it up for this fool sport.

(TOAD reenters with a clean Styrofoam cup. He displays it.)

TOAD: Concession stand. Millie give it t'me.

ZIGGIE: That's usin' yer noodle, Toad. I was relatin' to Candy Speed's true love for this game.

TOAD: Him an' his car was one.

ZIGGIE: Like…welded together.

CANDY: Speed sounds a bit kinky t'me.

P A: *(Off)* Sorry, L A, yer off by a whisker.

TOAD: *(Shouting)* SORRY, L A. *(Afterthought)* SORRY LARD ASS! *(Proudly laughing)*

CANDY: You talk big when you can't be heard.

(Four others have entered undetected from upstage. They have more booze. The women are attractive though GLENNA RAE is a bit disheveled. BO PEEP carries a guitar. RICKY wears a lightweight, sleeveless denim jacket. Inscribed on the back: "When I Die I'll Go To Heaven Since I've Spent My Time In Hell—Iraq, 2003-06". Finally, SLICK is a sunglasses-macho guy, fairly imposing as befits a former football star. They all wear clothes and hair that the townsfolk deem more appropriate elsewhere. Hell, perhaps)

(Quietly, GLENNA RAE approaches CANDY from behind then screeches in her ear.)

GLENNA RAE: EEEEEK!!!

(CANDY and TOAD are unnerved. ZIGGIE stares at happy-go-lucky RICKY. CANDY heads after GLENNA RAE but she slips away, laughing.)

CANDY: BITCH!!!

(Suddenly, GLENNA RAE wheels to meet CANDY's challenge. CANDY halts and TOAD intercedes by holding CANDY. She shakes him off vehemently.)

(All of this should seem fairly routine for all parties.)

CANDY: *(To TOAD)* Don't you touch me again. *(To GLENNA RAE)* You coulda made me deaf.

GLENNA RAE: I'd have done you a favor. You'd never hafta hear yourself talk again.

TOAD: Damn, Glenna Rae. You scared the shit outta me.

GLENNA RAE: If that were true we'd be up to our necks.

BO PEEP: Governor declare a state of emergency. "RECORD SHIT STORM HITS STATE!"

(There's a general round of camaraderie except CANDY *for* GLENNA RAE *and* ZIGGIE *for* RICKY.*)*

TOAD: *(To* RICKY*)* Hey, dude…

RICKY: Jeez-uss Toad, what happened to you?

TOAD: *(Proudly)* Fight club.

GLENNA RAE: Jeez, did you win?

BO PEEP: Does he look like he won?

CANDY: You gonna sing some, Bo?

BO PEEP: For myself. Not for you assholes.

RICKY: *(Indicating* SLICK*)* Hey Zig, look who we picked up.

ZIGGIE: *(Enthusiastically)* Nah, you can't lift that big a load of shit.

(A "brotherly" handshake and friendly roughhouse between the ex-high school football co-captains.)

SLICK: Hey Zig, how's it hangin', boy?

ZIGGIE: I'm doin' great, ole buddy. *(To the others)* Where'd you find this bastard?

RICKY: 7-11. We were buyin' beer.

GLENNA RAE: There was ole Slick with his raggedy-ass posse. We told him we were rendezvousin' with his ole teammate and he jumped aboard.

ZIGGIE: *(Good-naturedly)* Teammate! I took alla lumps an' Slick got alla glory.

SLICK: Biggest problem I had runnin' was stumblin' over you.

(Everyone laughs including ZIGGIE. *They toast, drink, smoke(?). When* GLENNA RAE *passes the bottle to him…)*

ZIGGIE: Where you been? Years since you seen Speed an' you come late an' drunked-up t'boot.

GLENNA RAE: Maybe I don't care about him anymore.

ZIGGIE: Maybe you're scared how much you do.

GLENNA RAE: An' I'm not drunk.

ZIGGIE: Not yet. But it's still mornin'.
Who's got my stash?

(RICKY *produces a pocket-sized pouch.*)

GLENNA RAE: Maybe I don't need an old lover when I got a pair of young ones.

(GLENNA RAE *feints seductively to* RICKY *and* SLICK...*fun all around.*)

CANDY: Is that separately or together?

GLENNA RAE: It's better than none at all. You'll find that out when Ziggie decides he's had en—

ZIGGIE: YOU TWO SHUT UP!!! Drownin' out the damn machines.

P A: (*Off*) An' now an ole favorite from Walla Walla, Washington. Drivin' his Coyote Q22...MACKIE MILLER!!!

TOAD: Hey, Mackie Miller, Zig. An' his Coyote Q-twenty-somethin'. (*He bellows an irritating Coyote howl.*)

(ZIGGIE *gestures to* RICKY *who tosses the pouch from hand to hand.* ZIGGIE *approaches and* RICKY *throws the pouch to him.* ZIGGIE *opens it and checks.*)

ZIGGIE: Who's been inta this shit?

GLENNA RAE: Bo Peep, what d'you know about this travesty of justice?

BO PEEP: You know me, Glenna. I'm innocent. Pure as the driven snow.

(Hoots all around except for ZIGGIE*)*

BO PEEP: *(Coyly)* Only a figure of speech.

(The car takes off and roars past. All but ZIGGIE *turn to watch [but with no great enthusiasm].)*

ZIGGIE: How 'bout you, Slick?

*(*SLICK *just shakes his head.)*

ZIGGIE: Ooops, sorry. It wouldn't be you. I hear you're dealin', yerself.

BO PEEP: Owww…come over here, Slick. Sit by me, brother.

GLENNA RAE: I know who did it but I'm not talkin'.

RICKY: Bullshit, Glenna. You'll talk as soon as our backs are turned.

*(*RICKY *swigs from the bottle until* ZIGGIE *grabs it and the wine dribbles.)*

ZIGGIE: Thanks, pal.

(All freeze as the tension mounts. ZIGGIE *methodically wipes the rim clean and swigs.)*

RICKY: I hafta ask why you're the custodian since we all threw in equal.

ZIGGIE: I made the connection.

*(*ZIGGIE *wipes the near-empty bottle under his armpit and returns it to* RICKY*. His bluff emphatically called,* RICKY *hands the bottle to* TOAD *who wavers on a swig but then declines. But in time he'll pour the last of the contents into his own cup.)*

ZIGGIE: You suggestin' I'm rippin' off?

GLENNA RAE: *(Mischievously)* Toad did.

TOAD: *(Panicky)* No, I didn't, Zig. She's a lyin' bitch.

(Laughter from all but ZIGGIE*.)*

ZIGGIE: Y'all don't appreciate the trouble I go to. I pro-
cure the best stuff around for you.

BO PEEP: 'Cept maybe for Mister Slick over here.

P A: *(Off)* Nice ride, Mackie. Ya got eight-tenths of a
second t'spare.

TOAD: 'Nother qualifier.

BO PEEP: You're a qualifier for the pig farm.

(The women snort and oink at him.)

ZIGGIE: 'Member our agreement? I take the risks, I hold
the goods. I get busted, I take the rap.

TOAD: Why're you so good to us?

ZIGGIE: 'Cause you're like little kids. You need
someone to wipe yer snotty noses.

*(BO PEEP and GLENNA RAE go through a faux ritual of
wiping one another's noses. ZIGGIE ignores them.)*

TOAD: We ain't kids no more, Zig.

ZIGGIE: I'm in charge. Maybe that's just the order of
things. Hey Slick, Mookie Morgan says he bought
some grass from you. Says it was like somethin'
between Toad's toes.

(Laughter, hoots. TOAD smiles slightly.)

ZIGGIE: Now, I suggest we relax an' take in the action.

TOAD: Hey Slick, gimmee a toothpick.

RICKY: Give us all a toothpick, Slick.

*(SLICK produces a small lode of toothpicks wrapped in tissue
and distributes to the men only. ZIGGIE tosses his and
SLICK retains it as if it had value. BO PEEP gestures for it
but she's ignored.)*

SLICK: Ain't ladylike.

*(RICKY, SLICK and TOAD go through a ritual of tearing the
tissues, inserting the 'picks and then savoring the flavor.*

This should be done simultaneously but not in unison. The women watch in bemusement.)

TOAD: Ummm. Mint.

BO PEEP: Whatta you guys need toothpicks for? You ain't just eaten.

TOAD: So what we ain't just eaten?

BO PEEP: They're for diggin' grub outta yer choppers.

TOAD: Naw.

BO PEEP: Then what're they for?

TOAD: Nothin' you'd understand.

Hey, I aint a kid. I'm a man.

BO PEEP: A kid's a baby billygoat. That's you…rootin' through the garbage.

TOAD: I'm just lookin' for my silver. *(Indicating his silver foil ball)*

BO PEEP: What are you gonna do with that silver? Open up a jewelry store?

TOAD: Silver *foil.*

My granddaddy tole me that in World War Two folks got paid for turnin' this in. Maybe soon in the war—

RICKY: They need more than tin foil in Eye-raq.

ZIGGIE: Reckon so, Rick. You're the authority.

CANDY: You oughtta know, boy.

(An awkward pause as RICKY seethes. Then…)

CANDY: This is the life.

GLENNA RAE: Sittin' here in the old speedway.

TOAD: Oval.

GLENNA RAE: Yeah, oval. Why d'they call it an oval, Toad?

TOAD: *(Shrugs)* Cause it's shaped round, I guess.

GLENNA RAE: Why don't they just call it a zero, then?

BO PEEP: "Here comes Speed Larsen around the ole zero."

GLENNA RAE: Hey Zig, when is Speed's time trial comin' up?

TOAD: They's savin' the best for last.

RICKY: *(To ZIGGIE)* So how come you worried about us? Just cause we were A-WOL when they opened today.

BO PEEP: He wasn't worried about us.

RICKY: Hey Bo, Zig cares about us when we got somethin' of his.

ZIGGIE: You got that right, Ricky Roo.

CANDY: God, I gotta stay straight this weekend.

BO PEEP: Fat chance.

GLENNA RAE: How?

CANDY: I didn't show up again last Monday. Ole Miz Wilcox gimmee hell. You know what a sarcastic bitch she can be.

GLENNA RAE: Tell me about it. I was in an' outta that job faster than a preacher in a whorehouse.

CANDY: Tuesday mornin' she greets me with... *(Mimicking with crossed eyes and buck teeth)* "Well, if it isn't Miss Florinda Terrell, Queen of The Quarry."

(Merriment all around)

P A: *(Off)* From...Bem...Bem... *(Evidently consulting a colleague)* How you say that, Sparky? *(Beat)* Bem-ij-ee? That's a new one on me. *(Back to his P A demeanor)* From Bemidji, Minnesota, drivin' his Super Mongoose 500, Freddy D Handy.

BO PEEP: *(Sarcastically)* Wow, a Super Mongoose.

GLENNA RAE: A Mongoose, a Coyote

CANDY: A Timber Wolf—

BO PEEP: A Panther—

GLENNA RAE: Is this a raceway or a zoo?

TOAD: I seen Wild Kingdom the other night. A leopard caught an antelope. Got him right inna jugular *(Pronounced "jug-ler")* How come you never see antelopes catch nothin'? No wonder they're so skinny. Did anyone see it on Wild Kingdom? *(No response, continuing…)* Ole Freddy D Handy. Saw him crasht once. T-boned near t'death.

RICKY: Maybe it'll happen again.

BO PEEP: That what you're wishin' for, Rick? Quench your appetite for violence.

RICKY: My appetite for violence is plenty quenched, Bo Peep. Or else I'd punch yer teeth out.

ZIGGIE: A crash is just part of the game. Ain't that what yer sayin', Bo?

BO PEEP: Seems t'me to be the *point* of the game.

ZIGGIE: So Bo, as an artist of the first water…you don't see any beauty out there? Any… color…you hear any rhythm? Harmony?

BO PEEP: Yeah, Ziggie. Speed Larsen is a real fuckin' Mozart.

CANDY: Hey, don't anyone wanna hear about me an' ole Mizz Wilcox?

GLENNA RAE: *(Ignoring her)* You gotta point, Zig. Speed's cousin is an artist. He painted that beautiful number 5 on his car.

RICKY: Frankie painted that?

TOAD: Frankie The Fairy?

(GLENNA RAE *just shakes her head.*)

(*The car starts up and all watch until it passes and the sound fades.*)

CANDY: Where was I?

TOAD: When?

CANDY: Last Tuesday morning.

TOAD: I dunno. The Paradise.

RICKY: "Queen of The Quarry".

CANDY: (*Satisfied, she'll imitate with comic enthusiasm*) So, ole Wilcox says, "I know it would be a staggerin' blow to Sam's Club but you should consider movin' on. Spend your leisure at your quarry retreat with your sophisticated friends."

TOAD: (*Dopey grin*) "Sophisticated". That's us, arright.

CANDY: So, y'know what I sez t'her?

BO PEEP: Didn't anyone bring any music?

RICKY: That's what *you're* for, Bo.

BO PEEP: Geez, what a pack a'limp-dicked deadbeats. We could be listenin' t'some good music all the time we're waitin'.

TOAD: There's music in them motors, Bo. Songs in them screechin' tires.

BO PEEP: (*Staring at* TOAD) You believe what you just said?

TOAD: Not really. But it sounds good. Huh, Zig?

P A: (*Off*) And Freddy D Handy makes it just under the wire.

ZIGGIE: He ain't a threat.

CANDY: (*A lull, then striking…*) So I sez, "Mizz Wilcox, you oughtta truck yer boney ass out there some time. Maybe after yer Sunday mornin' Bible class. Get yerself stoned, do a little skinny-dippin'. Hook up with a few guys." Then y'know what I said t'her? (*No interest, thus no response.* YOU BASTARDS KNOW WHAT I TOLE HER???

GLENNA RAE: Sure, you told her to fuck off.

CANDY: (*Liking what she's heard*) Glenna Rae, you're psychic. The exact same thing you said to her ratty face a while back. I said it loud an' clear. Then I added, "I betcha Sam Walmart wouldn'ta had no problem with me." Then I turned on my heel and went behind my cosmetic counter.

GLENNA RAE: Honey, you know that's a bold-faced lie.

CANDY: It's the truth, Glenna Rae. God's honest.

GLENNA RAE: Swear it on your momma, girl. C'mon, get your hand up.

CANDY: I don't do such a thing.

GLENNA RAE: *You* don't swear?

CANDY: Not on my momma. I may swear <u>at</u> her but—

RICKY: Whoo-ee…whoo-ee…whoo-ee! Getting' high… gettin' high.

TOAD: Cause you didn't sleep last night, Rick.

RICKY: If I did you'd have tried to get in Bo Peep's drawers.

BO PEEP: He'd have wound up with a herniated rupture.

TOAD: Bullhockey!

RICKY: I gotta take me a leak.

ZIGGIE: You sure you're O K, Rick?

RICKY: (*Heading off*) Long way t'go.

GLENNA RAE: All downhill for you.

RICKY: You'll be there when I hit rock bottom, Glenna. *(Exits)*

ZIGGIE: *(With deliberation)* Yeah, I gotta go myself.

(GLENNA RAE eyes ZIGGIE suspiciously.)

ZIGGIE: *(Defensively to GLENNA RAE)* Hey, when ya gotta go...

(ZIGGIE leaves the binocs with CANDY, kisses her and heads off. She follows his departure via the glasses.)

P A: *(Off)* Now, from Dearborn, Michigan, drivin' a Prairie Dog V-50, MIZZ Judy McCandless.

(BO PEEP and GLENNA RAE shriek with glee.)

GLENNA RAE: Owwwweeeee! YOU GO, GIRL!!!

BO PEEP: KICK ASS, JUDY!

TOAD: Hey, here she is, Slick.

SLICK: Shee-ittttt.

(BO PEEP grabs the binocs from CANDY, peers, then hands them to GLENNA RAE who peers.)

GLENNA RAE: Gutsy girl.

CANDY: Yeah, I guess.

TOAD: She's cool.

CANDY: I dunno. Seems kinda strange...a girl drivin'.

TOAD: Wonder if Speed knows this babe.

SLICK: Betcha Speed's screwin' 'er.

TOAD: Betcha they's all screwin' 'er.

(SLICK and TOAD revel in this comment, of course.)

TOAD: *(To GLENNA RAE)* Can I see?

(GLENNA RAE offers the glasses to BO PEEP but she declines. Then she gives them to TOAD. CANDY scampers to share with him.)

TOAD: She looks like all the rest with that face mask.

SLICK: *(Coming alive, he commandeers the glasses)* Well, she ain't like all the others. *(Adjusts the focus)* What's wrong with this focus?

BO PEEP: Focus isn't off, Slick. You just have fuzzy vision. Always did.

SLICK: I got nothin' against girls competin'. Only they should be against each other.

GLENNA RAE: Divide an' conquer with you, huh?

BO PEEP: Y'know, I always thought women were too smart for racin' cars.

SLICK: It's just the principle of the thing.

GLENNA RAE: You were always big on principles, Slick.

(McCandless is off, to universal attention.)

TOAD: She's doin' pretty good.

SLICK: But hell, she's out there by herself. No competition.

BO PEEP: Still, she gotta zip around to the nut wavin' the tablecloth.

SLICK: But she'll fold in the race tomorra.

TOAD: I dunno, Slick. She might just outfox those boys.

BO PEEP: Not a tall order.

GLENNA RAE: Yeah, my relationship with Speed did not tax the intellect.

BO PEEP: *(Goodnaturedly)* Mostly who does what to who and how. Huh. Glenna?

(Hi-five between BO PEEP and GLENNA RAE. ZIGGIE re-enters, sees them all focused on the track and hustles to a vantage point.)

ZIGGIE: Speed?

TOAD: Nah, it's the girl.

ZIGGIE: *(Dismayed)* Z'at all?

TOAD: Z'at all? This could be history today.

GLENNA RAE: Whatta you know about history?

TOAD: First woman racer at this track. An' if she should win—

(The next four lines simultaneously:)

ZIGGIE: She ain't gonna win.

GLENNA RAE: She's gonna win.

SLICK: No way.

BO PEEP: You go, girl.

ZIGGIE: Truth be told, I fear for this girl. She's up against some pretty mean boys tomorra. They'd put her against a wall t'save face.

GLENNA RAE: First they gotta catch her.

P A: *(Off. Lethargically)* McCandless qualifies.

(The woman cheer. TOAD refers to the watch.)

TOAD: Qualifies, hell! She got the best time so far.

(TOAD claps, whistles, stomps then desists when he realizes that SLICK and ZIGGIE aren't with him.)

ZIGGIE: A month ago I went down to Ellisville. There was an ad for a mechanic in the paper.

TOAD: You leavin' Shorty's?

ZIGGIE: I didn't say that. *(Mildly threatening)* An' don't you say I did.

TOAD: *(Mock-military salute)* Shorty won't know. Lips are sealed.

ZIGGIE: I'll get axed if Shorty hears I'm shoppin' around.

So, this garage was built from the ground up. Beautiful. Had four lifts, four pits. Buncha fuckin' computers. So I walk in an' ask for T R Gillespie. An this lady behind the desk—

SLICK: T R Gillespie.

ZIGGIE: How'd you know?

SLICK: My brother answered the ad.

ZIGGIE: Woman's a fuckin' engineer. Took her degree to the bank an' they bought her pitch. Her husband's head mechanic but she's head honcho.

TOAD: He's pussy-whupped.

ZIGGIE: They got eighteen mechanics…an some *are women!!!*

BO PEEP: Gimmee that address. I know cars.

ZIGGIE: Forget it. They're all computer geeks…some from college. She asks if I know computers. I sez, "No, I know cars, I'm a real mechanic". She sez, "Forget it, no on-the-job trainin'.

TOAD: But alla your years at Shorty's—

ZIGGIE: Don't count for shit. The Shortys of this world been passed by.

TOAD: Not me. I'm getting' outta here. Gonna get rich.

ZIGGIE: The world's got our balls in her pocket.

Speed saw it comin'. He saw the light. He made his move…he made it through.

TOAD: Yes, sir. He reached for the gold ring an' nabbed it. Like on the carousel at Hunt's Park.

GLENNA RAE: It's a brass ring at Hunt's Park.

CANDY: An' it's a merry-go-round.

(RICKY *staggers on, his lip bloodied. He holds his side. All save* ZIGGIE *express concern.)*

GLENNA RAE:	TOAD:	BO PEEP:
Ricky!	Jee-zuss!	Holy shit!

CANDY: *(Rushing to support him)* What happened, Rick?

GLENNA RAE: *(To ZIGGIE)* Whatta you know about this?

ZIGGIE: I don't tend t'Ricky Roo. Anythin' coulda happened in his condition. Coulda fell. Coulda pissed on some dude's shoes an' got hisself clocked.

GLENNA RAE: You did a number on him...on a disabled vet.

ZIGGIE: Rickie can still duke. Besides, I don't do numbers on punks.

BO PEEP: He wasn't a punk in Eye-raq. Took a land mine for us.

ZIGGIE: True. Rick was a hero. We're beholden t'him. But this here's America. *(To RICKY)* I didn't touch him. Rick, tell these girls straight out—

RICKY: *(Seething but honor-bound)* Stoned...shouldna drank so fast. I stumbled.

P A: *(Off Starting to sound a bit drunk)* This here's Duane Fields from "Chuly Vista", California.... Drivin' a ... drivin' ...le's see here...a Killershark Unlimited, Sure. What the hell else would he be drivin'?

ZIGGIE: See, Glenna Rae? What'd I tell ya?

CANDY: C'mon girls, let's get him down t'first-aid.

(BO PEEP helps her. SLICK and TOAD don't.)

GLENNA RAE: You mind if I stay, girls? Y'know, in case Speed—

CANDY: *(Lugging RICKY and with a bit of bitchiness)* It's O K honey, even if he won't remember you.

ZIGGIE: *(To SLICK and TOAD)* Hey, you two give our ole buddy a hand. Where's your compassion for yer fella man?

TOAD: Ain't got none.

ZIGGIE: Well you better get some, boy. You give us gentlemen a bad name.

(SLICK *and* TOAD *cross and—sort of—help as they head off.*)

CANDY: Don't hurt him.

TOAD: He's arready hurt, dumbass.

(They exit. Pause)

GLENNA RAE: You didn't hafta do that.

ZIGGIE: Those boys take you women for granted. They shoulda been helpin' Ricky. What are friends for?

GLENNA RAE: Cut the crap, Zig. You're not talkin' to Candy.

ZIGGIE: I tole ya, Glenna...an Ricky tole ya—

GLENNA RAE: Cause he copped a little of yer stash?

ZIGGIE: Rick's gettin' too big for his britches. A Purple Heart don't give you a pass.

GLENNA RAE: It wouldn'a happened if he was able-bodied.

(ZIGGIE is cut short by this. It's a truth he doesn't want to hear. It's all he can do to keep from exploding but he has a grudging respect for GLENNA RAE above all the others. After a pause...)

ZIGGIE: How come yer concerned about Rick? You tryna resurrect your high school romance?

GLENNA RAE: "Res*urrect*" is not possible after Rick's land mine "misfortune". My love for Rick is strictly platonic. Nowadays, he's just *there*...like Toad...like Slick.

ZIGGIE: Y'know, Ricky was sayin' that Speed's spooked since he crashed at Daytona.

GLENNA RAE: I know he's scared.

ZIGGIE: What???

GLENNA RAE: Speed's father told me. Handwritin's on the wall. His times are fallin' off. Hell, he's been fifteen years on the circuit. Damn near got himself killed two years ago.

ZIGGIE: Then why's he riskin' his butt on a dinkey-ass track like this? I mean, he was at Indianapolis in May.

GLENNA RAE: Broke down. Didn't finish.

ZIGGIE: *(Overly defensive)* He didn't break down. His engine—

GLENNA RAE: Speed broke down. His dad says it was fatigue…nervous exhaustion. Curly says he's hopin' the Hinochi Motor Company will set him up with a franchise.

ZIGGIE: Hell, Speed's no businessman.

GLENNA RAE: He'll just be the front. They'll hire a manager. Speed'll just shake hands and shoot the shit. They'll fly him to Japan once in a while to test a new car.

ZIGGIE: Japan, huh? That's what Ricky fought for? A Jap car maker?
Speed wants to come back here? After all he's seen… all he's done?

GLENNA RAE: He'll be a big turd in a small cesspool.

(ZIGGIE stares and GLENNA RAE reverts a bit.)

GLENNA RAE: A metaphor, Zig. Bad example. This is beautiful country. Really. 'Cept for its underbelly.

ZIGGIE: "Underbelly"? Is that supposed t'be us?

GLENNA RAE: Depends who's labelin'.
Speed's broke. That mansion he was buildin' for his daddy still stands half-finished.

ZIGGIE: Damn, we're wantin' to get out an' he's wantin' back in.

GLENNA RAE: How much are we "wantin'"?
So, I'm playin' a long shot. If I get to see him...see how he still feels about me after ten years...I think he wants to settle down with a fine woman.

ZIGGIE: That'd be you, Glenna Rae. *(Smiles)* On a good day.

GLENNA RAE: *(Smiles back)* Shut up, you.
I'd like that. Clean up my act. Have kids. Raise a family. I'd like motherin'. Hell, all I've got t'look forward to around here is my Golden Age Discount Card.

ZIGGIE: Hell, you were jailbait back then.

GLENNA RAE: He still remembers. He still asks Curly about me.

ZIGGIE: Why does he ask his father? Why doesn't he ask you?

GLENNA RAE: My first time was with Speed. Sort of a birthday present from my brother. L. Henry told me that Speed Larsen was out in the garage... just waitin'. I never hesitated. Hit the sky that night. Haven't been back since he drove outta town.

ZIGGIE: Ain't cause you ain't been tryin'.

GLENNA RAE: If I can't be with the one I love, I can be at the quarry with a few that I like.

P A: *(Off)* From Flagstaff, Arizona drivin' that flashy Chicken Hawk V *(pro, "Vee")* —

MALE VOICE: *(Off)* Five. Chicken Hawk Five.

P A: *(Off)* Well why don't they just write "five". Let's hear it for Davey Long.

ZIGGIE: You're above slingin' hash at the Camelot Diner. What happened t'your acting? You were a star in high school.

GLENNA RAE: And you were my male counterpart.

ZIGGIE: Me? I wasn't an actor.

GLENNA RAE: Oh yes you were, Zig.

ZIGGIE: That *Glass Menagerie*…that was some playactin'. LaShanna Davis couldn't'a done better.

GLENNA RAE: LaShanna Davis? She was no actress.

ZIGGIE: No, but she *had* M S.

GLENNA RAE: It came natural for me.

ZIGGIE: I'll say. A crazy mother and a fucked-up brother. You only hadda learn the lines.

GLENNA RAE: An' stiffen my leg. The rest was *déjà vu*.

ZIGGIE: You shoulda finished college.

GLENNA RAE: College was more a curse than a blessing. I started right off playing lead roles. Freshman year. "What's to prove", I asked myself. So I hightailed it off to New York. But I was ill-prepared. I auditioned for everything. But all I got were small roles in bad plays at shithole spaces. I'd take acting lessons from failed actors. I hadda live cheap. Downtown. I fell in with a bad crowd…bad habits.

ZIGGIE: Just like us.

GLENNA RAE: No, not like you guys. You wouldn't let me hurt myself. But *they* did the hurting.

ZIGGIE: You picked the wrong city. Maybe you and I should get outta here…go someplace together. Someplace with opportunities.

GLENNA RAE: What about Candy?

ZIGGIE: She'll never leave.

GLENNA RAE: For you, she will.

ZIGGIE: It wouldn't be anything between us. We'd just be…partners. Take care of each other.

GLENNA RAE: No doubt. I once thought that we'd be an ideal pair. But only if you were a different person. Why don't you leave on your own?

ZIGGIE: *(Uncomfortable with this)* Like you said, it's tough breakin' into a strange place.

GLENNA RAE: In a *strange* place, you'd be right at home. Run for mayor. Win hands down.

ZIGGIE: If it doesn't work out with you an' Speed …

GLENNA RAE: You certainly wouldn't get bored after this place. No more super job at Shorty's. No more spare change riflin' his candy machine.

(By now GLENNA RAE and ZIGGIE are casually and innocently draped on the seats, his arm around her neck.)

ZIGGIE: Remember my first car? '89 Cougar 300. We'd pile inta it on Friday nights an' drive a couple hundred miles. Only in a thirty mile radius. Cruisin' all night… back an' forth—

GLENNA RAE: —east and west—

ZIGGIE: —north an' south—

GLENNA RAE: —like rats in a maze.

Nothin' personal. Figure of speech.

Lou Jean is drivin' Momma crazy all over again. She's gone from Friday night 'til Monday morning when she stops in for her school books. She tells me, "We eat, sleep an' screw in cars. What kinda crummy existence is that?" So I says, "I been there. An' I made it through." She just laughs in contempt an' walks out the door.

CANDY: *(Re-entering)* Well, looka here. Hope I ain't bustin' anythin' up by my intrudin'.

GLENNA RAE: Nothin' that can't be reestablished once your back is turned.

CANDY: Don't doubt that of you, Glenna.

ZIGGIE: Candy, me'n Glenna Rae wanna hook up we could do it in private.

CANDY: Glenna Rae's been known t'do it front of appreciative audiences.

GLENNA RAE: You've been known to do it *with* appreciative audiences.

(CANDY goes for GLENNA RAE but ZIGGIE intervenes. GLENNA RAE giggles as things cool.)

ZIGGIE: How's Ricky comin' along?

CANDY: As if you cared. *(Pouts momentarily)*

ZIGGIE: I care. Rick's my main man.

CANDY: Nurse is fixin' him.
Hey, you two won't guess who I just seen.

GLENNA RAE: Elvis? You saw Elvis drinkin' 'Yoo Hoo" an' eatin' "Funny Bones".

CANDY: C'mom.

GLENNA RAE: I give up.

CANDY: You give up, Zig?

ZIGGIE: *(Weaarily)* You bet, Candy.

CANDY: Well, I wish you'd keep guessin' but...I SEEN CHARLENE DRAKE!!!

GLENNA RAE: You're kiddin'.

CANDY: Am not.

GLENNA RAE: True. You're not sharp enough to make things up.

ZIGGIE: I thought we seen the last of her.

CANDY: No such luck. She's back an' with a *husband.* An' guess what about him?

GLENNA RAE: Give up, Candy. So does Zig.

CANDY: Today's my day for stumpin'.
Well, Charlene's got herself hitched to an English*man*.

P A: *(Off)* And Davey Lane of Flagstaff, Arizona is another qualifier. *(Beat)* Wha...yeah, Davey Long, folks. Shorry about that, Davey.

ZIGGIE: Charlene always thought she was too good for anyone hereabouts.

CANDY: Not exactly. She chased after you like a bitch in heat, Zig.

GLENNA RAE: Yeah, alla her high-fallutin' ways went south with Ziggie.

CANDY: Her an' her fat ole Daddy's money.

GLENNA RAE: Her little red sports car.

CANDY: Summers in Europe.

GLENNA RAE: Ivy League college.

CANDY: Hey Glenna, you were twice as smart as her at Regional. Hell, even Bo was smarter. An' let's not forget my scholarship to State.

GLENNA RAE: *(Dismissively)* Cheerleadin'.

CANDY: Maybe I shoulda gone.

GLENNA RAE: They didn't offer cosmetology.

CANDY: Hey, if I went I wouldn't be takin' alla this shit from you two. You didn't usta be this way. If I knew all the abuse I'd be takin', I wouldna dyed my hair blonde. *(To* ZIGGIE*)* Charlene's daddy woulda killed you 'cept Charlene woulda killed him.

ZIGGIE: She changed any?

CANDY: Nah, a leopard don't change 'er stripes. I said, "Why Charlene, what brings the likes of you back here?" She says, "Daddy's ailin'.

(ZIGGIE *pumps his fist in quiet jubilation.*)

GLENNA RAE: Hope it's nothin' curable.

CANDY: "An I thought I'd show my man the local color." I sez, "Go to East End. See lotsa color there." An' she turns an' sez, "See what I mean, Rudolph?"

ZIGGIE: Only Rudolph I ever heard of was a reindeer.

CANDY: There was Rudolph Valentino.

GLENNA RAE: Rudolf Nureyev.

CANDY: (*After a blank stare*) Now, about Charlene… Understand, I ain't obsessed with gossip. However, this is fact*oid*. An' since Ziggie's curious about his ole trash bag—

ZIGGIE: Hey! We had a mutual…

GLENNA RAE: Respect?

ZIGGIE: No, understanding. We were off-limits to one another.

GLENNA RAE: *You* were *more* off-limits.

ZIGGIE: Yeah. I dragged her down an' she loved it. Folks never saw that side of her. We were mismatched, personally. But the animal stuff kept us goin'. 'At's the way t'have it.

CANDY: (*Quietly*) You feel that way about…

ZIGGIE: Nah. You an' me, Candy…we're in tune.

CANDY: "In tune". I like that. (*She initiates a snuggle.*)

GLENNA RAE: Aren't you a cute pair?

CANDY: And ain't you a jealous spinster-to-be? Incidentally, I tole Charlene you were up here but she declined a social call.

GLENNA RAE: *(To* ZIGGIE*)* You and her old man could compare notes.

CANDY: Me'n Charlene could compare notes.

GLENNA RAE: *(To* ZIGGIE*)* That limey's the benefactor of your perverse imagination.

(SLICK *leads* TOAD *back on by a spool of gauze wrapped around the latter's face.* TOAD *moans in mock-pain. Then he spins…spins…spins free of the binding. When he unravels…)*

TOAD: It's me! Carlton Pine!

(BO PEEP *and* RICKY *follow them on.* RICKY's *lip is repaired. He totes a cooler of beer.)*

TOAD: We miss anythin'?

GLENNA RAE: No, and we didn't miss you.

CANDY: You missed…ya gotta guess who you miss—

ZIGGIE: Charlene Drake.

CANDY: Aw Zig, you hadda go an'—

BO PEEP: CHARLENE! That bitch. She still doin' the "hurt dance"?

ZIGGIE: She's married to a British guy named Rudolph.

P A: *(Off)* Introducin' Gunther Sherman from Chambersburg, Pennsylvania, drivin' a PL8 Lightnin' Bug.

ZIGGIE: How you doin' boy?

RICKY: I need a drink.

ZIGGIE: You're O K, then.

(RICKY *digs out a beer as a car takes off.)*

TOAD: This place ain't fillin' up so good for Speed.

GLENNA RAE: It's only the trials. Wait'll the real thing tomorra.

(Suddenly, the screech of a skidding car. The group bolts to life. They freeze, focused forward. When the screech subsides, they relax.)

TOAD: Whoooooeeeee! Nearly had one that time.

P A: *(Off)* Shteady there, boy! Just a lil' bit of a tailshpin, folks.

RICKY: Alla way from Pennsylvania to get knocked out in the time trial.

BO PEEP: Wish I could get to Pennsylvania. They got music opportunities in Pittsburg... Philadelphia.

GLENNA RAE: You could take Ronette.

CANDY: Or you could leave her with me.

BO PEEP: With *you*? When pigs fly. You feed her popcorn and soda pop.

CANDY: *(Proudly positioning her body)* Never hurt me. Developed my body.

GLENNA RAE: Corroded your brain.

BO PEEP: If I was born a generation ago I coulda gone to Detroit. Got in with Motown.

RICKY: You *were* born a generation ago.

BO PEEP: Huh? Oh, yeah. If I'd been born a generation earlier, I coulda joined Motown.

GLENNA RAE: You could still be a big star, Bo. Come back to visit us when you're on top.

BO PEEP: What in hell for?

CANDY: If you have so little regard for us why don'tcha hang out with your own kind.

GLENNA RAE: Don't start that ignorant shit, Candy.

BO PEEP: Y'know Candy, that comment makes you sound like some ole cracker bitch.

CANDY: It does? Well, I'm certainly not that. Sorry, Bo. You're one of us. At least you're half-white.

(BO PEEP *nods acceptance of* CANDY's *apology.*)

BO PEEP: *(Quiet aside) Young* cracker bitch.

CANDY: You'll make folks forget about Marsha Enright.

BO PEEP: My momma won't mind the kid. *(Mimicking)* "The day you come home with that bit in yer belly was the day you bound your ties to 'er. You disgrace me then expect me to care for that poor creature."

CANDY: "Creature"? Ronette's beautiful. Your momma oughtta cherish her. She broke yer family's ugly streak.

(CANDY *laughs.* BO PEEP *doesn't.*)

GLENNA RAE: At least your family didn't run you off the farm.

BO PEEP: Naturally. Who'd take care of the sheep.

GLENNA RAE: Havin' an illegitimate child is no disgrace. It's a diversion. Your mother's pissed cause you never I D-ed the father.

RICKY: No wonder. Ronette looks like yer brother.

(RICKY *laughs but no one takes him seriously.*)

P A: *(Off)* Let's have a hand for the veteran from Shpearfish, Shouth Dakota, Murray Hammond. Kick assh, Murray.

BO PEEP: Did you meet any music people in New York, Glenna?

GLENNA RAE: Sure, me'n Beyonce double-dated. Bruce Springsteen...Paul McCartney...

SLICK: I been to New York. Went to a rap concert at Madison Square Garden.

BO PEEP: An' what did you learn?

SLICK: Learned that Madison Square Garden is round.

You can perform in the streets, Bo. In the parks.

BO PEEP: Yeah, for free. Fuck that!

SLICK: For tips.

TOAD: You give 'em anythin', Slick?

SLICK: Shit, no. They weren't that good.

ZIGGIE: What else did you do up there?

SLICK: Rode the subways a lot. All around town an'
back to my brother's place. Hung out at Times Square.

BO PEEP: Is Times Square round?

SLICK: No, it's flat. Like your titties.

Went t'Harlem. Harlem's nice. It's no ghetto...no slum.

BO PEEP: You movin' there, Slickster?

SLICK: Hell, no. Too crowded. I'm a country boy. I went
into this very nice bar, y'know. More like a high-class
lounge. Bought a round of drinks for the brothers and
sisters. Nothin'. No thanks. No buyback. Sheee-ooooot.

BO PEEP: Were you wearin' your overalls?

SLICK: I always wear my overalls.
Played a lotta videos. Saw a lotta movies. Hundreds
of movie houses. Some all night long. Seen Coney
Island. Rode The Cyclone. Stood up all the way. Seen
Greenwich Village. They's all queers, there.

ZIGGIE: Hmmmmm. So what did you do about that,
Slick?

SLICK: Got the fuck out! Pronto!

GLENNA RAE: See the United Nations?

(SLICK *shakes his head.*)

TOAD: Why bother? We seen that movie in civics class.
'Member, Bo? Miz Graham made us watch it.

GLENNA RAE: Poor Miz Graham.

(TOAD improvises a noose with the stolen gauze and comically "hangs" himself, eyes popping and tongue extended. ZIGGIE kicks him, angrily.)

ZIGGIE: Hey, that's gross a'you, boy! It's on accounta assholes like you that she offed herself.

GLENNA RAE: Miz Graham believed in you. Believed in alla us. But especially believed in you.

TOAD: *(Suddenly humbled)* Yes...she did. *(He looks skyward and blesses himself)*

BO PEEP: You should be ashamed of yourself. Get over there, away from the rest of us.

(TOAD complies, moving towards the trash can.)

GLENNA RAE: Sit on that trash can. That's your spot. Your *toad*stool.

BO PEEP: You see the Statue of Liberty, Slickster?

SLICK: From a distance.

BO PEEP: Any plays?

(SLICK shakes his head.)

GLENNA RAE: Museums?

SLICK: The Bronx Zoo. That's a sorta animal museum. I went past the Modern Art Museum one day. They had pitchers in the lobby. It was twenty dollars to get in. But I wouldn't pay twenty dollars for one of those paintings.

GLENNA RAE: You're a real cultural butterfly, Slick.

RICKY: Hey Toad, when are you goin' t'the big city.

(It's "Toad Time", a periodic ritual that scapegoats the natural i.e. TOAD. He's come to accept his role as inevitable and with a goofy sense of pride.)

CANDY: Make that big name for yourself.

GLENNA RAE: You gonna leave inna Mercedes?

BO PEEP: Inna white van inna straight jacket?

ZIGGIE: Where're you gonna live when you're on top?

TOAD: I don't wanna leave. This here's a beautiful place. Lotta swell folks. But I might take me a visit to Sweden.

(Various "Sweden?"s).

BO PEEP: Where'd *that* come from?

TOAD: My cousin, Delmer tole me—

GLENNA RAE: "Delmer"? Do you mean, "Worm"?

P A: *(Off)* From Strasburg, Virginia, drivin' an' XDA Screamin' Vulture, Buddy Freeman.

TOAD: Yeah... Worm. But our family never—

RICKY: We're your real family, Toad. 'Member years ago, we took you two down t'the river an' re-baptized you?

GLENNA RAE: You came to the surface as "Toad".

BO PEEP: An' your cousin bobbed up as "Worm".

TOAD: Yeah. Anyways, Delm— ...uh, Worm learned about Swedish women in the navy. He says they're all beautiful an' they're all...*av-ail-a-bull.*

(The women "vamp" and swoon around TOAD.*)*

CANDY: Hey Bo, how bout that song?

TOAD: *(Irritated)* Aw come on...yer mockin' me.

CANDY: Mockin' you??? This here song is a tribute. A gen*uine* artist went an' composed a song for you an' you wanna delete it.

BO PEEP: I'm hurt, Toadster.

P A: *(Off)* Atta Boy, Freeman. Yer in t'shpare.

*(The others—*ZIGGIE *excepted—start to bang out the country-rock rhythms of* Toad's Song. *One may pull out*

a harmonica. Another bangs two beer cans together and another taps a penknife on a bottle. They stomp feet and everyone with free hands will clap. When they are into the beat, BO PEEP sings and strums as a makeshift circle forms around TOAD. Initially, he resents the ritual yet he savors the recognition and he slowly gives in to the rhythm of the number like some moronic deity.)

ZIGGIE *is the only non-participant. He remains furthest downstage while the others cavort. When he spots Speed, he stands on the bleachers. Only then will the song fade as the others rivet on the track.)*

*(*BO PEEP *is the featured singer. The others sing the chorus.)*

(Toad's Song)

If you ever take a wrong turn and stop in on my hometown,
Take a minute to discover you don't wanna hang around.
The people who talk friendly are rotten through and through,
But there's a guy you hafta meet cause he's too weird to be true.

(Chorus:)

Toad, Toad, remember his name.
Cause this ole boy is headed for the loser's Hall of Fame.
Toad, Toad, he's really outta sight.
His body's thin and dirty an' and his face is just a fright.

Well, my home folks are self-righteous as they talk their platitudes,
And when you come right down to it, they're narrow-minded prudes.
They'll gossip, curse and cheat you an' then point you down the road,

But the worst of them is twice as good as disgustin'
Mister Toad.

(Chorus repeated)

So when you think you've seen enough and you're
headed on your way,
Don't forget t'count your blessin's that you didn't hafta
stay.
Cause a godforsaken place like this you may live to see
once more.
But Toad's a thing you'll never see till you're at ole
Satan's door.

(Chorus repeated)

*(Into the final chorus, RICKY notices ZIGGIE and breaks from
the crowd. He reaches for the binocs but ZIGGIE brushes
him off. BO PEEP abandons the song into the last chorus.
But TOAD keeps ecstatically skipping in circles, eyes closed
and jaw agog. He is truly entranced until a few lines into
the announcement when he snaps out of it and rejoins the
others.)*

P A: *(Off. Sounding plenty drunk by now)* And here he
is, folksh...the guy we've all been waitin' for...the
international native shon an' namesake of this very
same racin' track, Mister Shpeed Larsen...

*(The men and GLENNA RAE go haywire hooting and
cheering as BO PEEP and CANDY surreptitiously satirize
them [CANDY to the point of a pseudo-orgasm]. TOAD
mimes a hand microphone as he plays the announcer. As he
cites the car's details, the others slowly pay amazed attention
to his new-found aptitude.)*

TOAD: ...drivin' his Super Special TP-78 Golden Tiger
Cat., with the dynamometer fantail outlet as well as the
turbo-charged 8.1 litre mid-engine featuring triple X19
cam shafts with free flow exhaust manifolds, silver-
studded radial traction grip masters and a high dead-

back axle ratio with three crown wheel and pinions, a lightened flywheel, piston-patterned shock absorbers, a steel drop arm, rack and pinion steering, front struts, zodiac running gear, Apollo linkage, vertical dampers, coil springs, tandem brake master cylinders…and a *Pioneer C D Player.*

GLENNA RAE: *(Amazed)* You are an idiot savant.

TOAD: Am like hell. I may not know much else but I know cars.

P A: *(Off)* Now our ole hometown boy will take one lap around the track before his run so's t'acknowledge his ole palsh. Then he'sh gonna line up for his time trial an' show us what the world's been witnesshin'. Sho, give him a wave when he passhes by.

(They follow Speed's approach from their left. They whistle, cheer, stomp…anything to get his attention. We hear cheering in the background. Using his glasses, ZIGGIE glows as Speed approaches. But his smile fades dramatically when Speed is dead in front of them. He lowers the glasses with a pole-axed expression. GLENNA RAE picks up on this and she snatches the glasses. She too, sees what ZIGGIE has determined before he grabs them back. Their argument is drowned out by the engine and the cheering. GLENNA RAE expresses vehement negation. ZIGGIE sits dejectedly as the others settle down and wait for the time trial.)

RICKY: Damn, gimmee a beer.

(Some go for beer but not ZIGGIE. GLENNA RAE is clearly tense and fetches a beer. BO PEEP notices.)

BO PEEP: It's only a man, honey.

TOAD: How's he look, Zig?

ZIGGIE: Good. Same as always.

BO PEEP: *(To GLENNA RAE)* Did he see us when he passed by, honey?

GLENNA RAE: He saw us. Didn't he, Ziggie?

TOAD: I thought I seen him wave, right Zig?

ZIGGIE: Y'might say that.

RICKY: Hey Bo, you think Speed could inspire a song in you?

BO PEEP: Happens I'm workin' one up. Speed's a real muse.

TOAD: *(Offended)* What'd you call him?

BO PEEP: A muse, you geek. A muse is an artist's inspiration.

TOAD: Y'mean, like "dope"?

CANDY: Dope is you. All you inspire is pity.

RICKY: Shut down yer pieholes. He's getting' ready t'lay rubber.

(ZIGGIE peers as we hear the motor in the distance. GLENNA RAE gestures towards ZIGGIE's binocs.)

GLENNA RAE: Ziggie, I wonder if I can—

ZIGGIE: Sorry Glenna, should'a brought yer own.

P A: *(Off)* Here goes, folksh. Billy Rae Jenks is getting' ready t'drop the checkered flag.

TOAD: Boy, I'm nervous. You nervous, Slick?

(SLICK shrugs and expressionless, shakes his head.)

TOAD: You cool, Slick. Cool as hell.

BO PEEP: Fire 'n ice, those boys.

P A: *(Off)* Ready, set...AND HE'S OFF!!!

(They all observe. GLENNA RAE is quietly intense. ZIGGIE watches through the binoculars. TOAD is the only one overly excited but all eyes are on the car. The noise becomes unbearable as the car passes. TOAD's shouts

of encouragement are drowned out. RICKY *is using the stopwatch.)*

TOAD: Owwww, c'mon, boy…ole Speed Larsen can do it for his fans…do it for ussss…for your hometown fans… We really need it, Speed… Burn the guts outta that machine… Do it for all of us…for Ziggie…an' Glenna Rae…an' Bo Peep…an' Candy…an' Slick…an' Ricky Roo… an' for me. Do it for me! FOR ME!! FOR ME!!!

(The noise abates when he drives past. All the following speakers focus on the track. The insults seem routine. GLENNA RAE *and* ZIGGIE *are stoic.)*

GLENNA RAE: How's he doin', Rick?

RICKY: Zero t'sixty in six.

CANDY: 'Zat good?

TOAD: Certainly it's good, ya dumb bitch.

CANDY: Don't you call me names, you ree-ree.

TOAD: I ain't no ree-ree.

CANDY: Are too.

TOAD: Am not.

GLENNA RAE: How's he doin', Rick?

RICKY: He's gonna make it.

BO PEEP: 'Zat all?

RICKY: *(Checking the watch)* No, not all. He's gonna break it. Gonna break the all-time track record. BREAK IT INNA THOUSAND PIECES!!!

(They start to chant [except for GLENNA RAE *and* ZIGGIE*]. They quickly build to a frenzy ["SPEED… SPEED… SPEED…SPEED'] until* RICKY *celebrates the record by pointing to the watch and jumping. They leap up, embrace, celebrate and for the most part, take their attention from the*

track. GLENNA RAE *and* ZIGGIE *are elevated a bit from the others.)*

(Suddenly, a terrific CRASH. All leap to the downstage wall area, save the fatalistic pair. The others are shocked as a flame effect catches their frozen expressions. A siren starts in the distance.)

P A: *(Off)* Great God Almighty!!!

(Fadeout)

END OF ACT ONE

ACT TWO

(Rural night sounds. Periodically, a dog barking)

(The stage is dimly lit save the illumination from two flashlights manipulated by CANDY *and* TOAD.)

(At rise, an automobile graveyard)

(The flashlight beams play from face-to-face to Speed's car [what's left of it]. The car could *be offstage. Strewn about are discarded car parts. If played proscenium or thrust, perhaps the backdrop can suggest the auto junk yard motif. If possible, a huge, blown-up photo of stacked wrecks.)*

CANDY: Poor sonofabitch never had a chance.

TOAD: Yeah, I had a hunch he was a goner.

CANDY: You're shrewd, Toad. Man bashes his car head-on into a concrete wall at a hundred and sixty M P H, flips over five times an' you had a notion he was cashin' out.

TOAD: Not a "notion". A "hunch".

CANDY: When were you *sure* he was worm bait? When the county coroner sent you a telegram?

TOAD: He don't even know me.

CANDY: *(Surveying the scene)* God, this place gimmee the creeperoos.

TOAD: How come? It ain't a *real* graveyard. It's a car graveyard.

CANDY: How come??? I'm out here with Speed dead an' you alive. If that ain't enough t'spook the shit outta ya...

TOAD: *(Sincerely)* You know I wouldn't hurt you.

CANDY: *(Beam offstage)* Where's Zig.

TOAD: Zig'll come back. Zig always comes back.

CANDY: *(Beam off)* Hey Toad, who belonged t'that ole T-bird?

TOAD: Oh, "Red Rocket".

CANDY: Who's he?

TOAD: The car was Red Rocket. Belonged to A O Purdy.

CANDY: Is A O Purdy in the happy huntin' ground? Or did he set out for greener pastures? *(She dials a number on her cell to no avail.)*

TOAD: You think he survived that? Got it up on 265. Lotsa folks were glad. Not me, though. He stripped that motha down, souped it back up, dropped the mufflers, then he'd barrel through town 'bout 3 A M wakin' alla babies. That's why they called him "Nightmare". *(Spookily)* A O "Nightmare" Purdy.

CANDY: Sonofabitch!

TOAD: Nah, just a good ole boy.

CANDY: *(Another beam offstage)* Ain't that Lula Grissom's Chevy over there?

TOAD: What's left of 'er. 'Member the night she stumbled outta The Paradise an' smacked inta those folks?

CANDY: She didn't smack inta them. Her car did.

TOAD: You gonna tell me that one about "Lefty's Fill'Er Up" an' the cigarettes?

(This controversial local tale triggers intimidating beams in each other's faces.)

CANDY: God's honest truth.

TOAD: God's truth and Lula's are two different things.

(During this speech TOAD *gestures* CANDY's *babbling and he quietly utters " blah, blah , blah...".)*

CANDY: Lula stopped at Lefty's for some butts and she was so drunk she forgot the emergency brake. That ole heap rolled back onna road an' killed those folks drivin' like their ass was on fire. *(Dramatically)* WHAM, BAM! That's all she wrote.

TOAD: You believe every half-ass rumor you hear?

CANDY: Weren't no rumor. I did some personal investigation on my own.

TOAD: Then how come Lefty told everybody that he seen it happen and that he helped her outta her car. It was a miracle she was only shook up some. That's what he tole Merle Hooper on The Sentinel. An' that's what he tole the court... that Lula was the victim.

CANDY: Damn! Everybody knows that Lula paid Lefty five hundred dollars to tell that boldfaced lie.

TOAD: BULL! Lefty's a church deacon.

CANDY: So was Lamar Wiley before he threw lye in his mother's face.

TOAD: If poor Lamar hadn't done it somebody else mighta.

CANDY: I swear you're the only one who believes that stuff an' nonsense t'this day.

TOAD: What about the jury, Miss Smartass?

CANDY: They felt sorry for Lula. Her car was totaled. An' she was drunk. It wasn't a purposeful act. An' the folks were outsiders. If they were local, y'know with kin an' all…

TOAD: *(Nods)* Different story.

CANDY: Damn straight.

TOAD: That sucks!

(A car is heard approaching.)

CANDY: Hey, somebody's comin'.

TOAD: Ricky Roo.

CANDY: How can ya tell?

TOAD: Hell girl, who else around here rolls with double camshaft an' twin glass packs.

(RICKY pulls up with a roar. Offstage lights illuminate the area and we become aware of some dismantling paraphernalia [tool box, crowbar, wrench, blowtorch, etc]. Four doors slam as the headlights go out and the stage goes dim. CANDY and TOAD point their beams off. They in turn, are illuminated by offstage beams. This manually-manipulated light show will continue until later when the stage is lit by RICKY's headlights.)

(It's clear that the newcomers have partied away their pain. They'll have booze in tow and at one point they'll break out the cocaine.)

TOAD: Hey Rick, how ya doin', boy?

BO PEEP: *(Entering with C D player and guitar)* You just left 'im, Toad. You think he come down with Alzheimers?

SLICK: *(Entering with a special handshake for TOAD)* How ya doin, dude?

TOAD: Ah'm O K.

RICKY: *(Entering)* Where's Ziggie?

BO PEEP: He left the quarry before us.

CANDY: *(Surprised)* The quarry? What'd he go back there for? *(Indicating* TOAD*)* When he dropped us off here he said he was goin' t'town for booze, bennies and butts. *(Strutting in imitation)* "Booze, bennies and' butts."

(Awkward silence from the newcomers.)

BO PEEP: He musta made a wrong turn.

CANDY: He knows this county like the back of—

(RICKY jumps on Speed's car [onstage or off].)

GLENNA RAE: *(Drunkenly)* I wish you'd have respect for the recently deceased, Rick.

RICKY: Like we'd say in Eye-raq, "What's dead is dead."

GLENNA RAE: I am a woman in mournin'.

RICKY: Bull-shittttt. You're a rock, Glenna.

GLENNA RAE: *(Surveying the wreck)* Damn, what a mess.

TOAD: 'At's what happens when ya hit a brick wall at a hundred-and-sixty M P H.

BO PEEP: Sensitivity's not your M O, Toad.

SLICK: Least he didn't suffer none.

GLENNA RAE: *(Skyward with a vengeance)* Thank you, God. Merciful Father, where are you comin' from? What's your weird agenda? What did we do to piss you off?

RICKY: Hey, Speed was a racin' man. He wouldn'a felt bitter about today.

GLENNA RAE: Don't talk like a moron. He got cheated outta half a lifetime. He's cheated in death, we're cheated in life.

BO PEEP: Hey Glenna, only a handful lived a fuller life. An' like you said, he did it in half the time.

GLENNA RAE: That's *not* what I said.

BO PEEP: He's a hero. Lived fast, died young. That's what it takes.

RICKY: Hey, Speed wouldn't want us mopin' like this. Hey Bo, how's that song you been workin' up for Speed?

BO PEEP: Pretty much the same number I was workin' on before the accident. I just changed the tense from alive t'dead.

RICKY: *(With a flourish)* Our own artist of the first water, Miss Lucinda "Bo Peep" Braxton has a musical tribute.

BO PEEP: *(Picking up her guitar)* Well, thank you Mister Ruane for that warm introduction. Now unnerstand kids, this thing ain't polished yet. I just banged it out while—

RICKY: It's the feelin' that counts, Bo.

BO PEEP: Well now, that's not quite true. Sometimes the meter is the most important—

RICKY: *(Impatient smile)* Play away, Bo.

BO PEEP: Ordinarily I gotta wait for the inspiration before—

RICKY: You need inspiration??? PLAY THE FUCKIN' SONG!!! THERE'S YOUR INSPIRATION!!!

BO PEEP: *(With a snarl towards* RICKY*)*This here's "Speed's Lament"

Speed Larsen came from my hometown, I'm awful proud t'say.
He was the fastest drivin' man in this whole U S A.
No other man would take such risks and wake up the next day.
But Speed was pure and he had God to guide him on his way.

*(The others nod assent or utter "Lovely"... "Touching"
except for cynical* GLENNA RAE.*)*

BO PEEP: *(To* GLENNA RAE*)* Pardon the reference to
God, Glenna.

One hot ole day not long ago, Speed drove back into
town.
The local folks were mighty pleased he hadn't let them
down.
For Speed had seen the world you see, he'd surely been
around.
But a humbler man you've never seen, even though he
wore the crown.

TOAD: What "crown"?

BO PEEP: The stage was set for Speed's big race, his was
the favored car.
Our hometown boy would win the day folks said from
near and far.
But fate had other plans for Speed an' despite a valiant
try,
Our hero's layin' rubber at that speedway in the sky.

*(*CANDY *whimpers.)*

BO PEEP: Now, here comes the chorus.

*(After "Sing it, girl" and "Solid gold" she rips into a
raucous rendition that is a duplicate of* Toad's Song *in ACT
ONE. The others turn and stare in disbelief as the rhythm
becomes recognizable.)*

BO PEEP: Speed, Speed, remember his name.
Cause this ole boy is headed for the winner's Hall of
Fame.
Speed, Speed was really outta sight.
His car was super-special and his heart was fulla fight.
Speed, Speed, remember his name.
Cause this ole boy is headed for the winner's Hall of
Fa—

RICKY: HEY, HEY, whatya call that?

BO PEEP: "Speed's Lament". Y'know, workin' title.

RICKY: Well you better be workin' harder..

TOAD: That's *my* chorus, Bo.

BO PEEP: I thought I could sneak it past you guys.

RICKY: Be easier sneakin' a freight train past us.

BO PEEP: I have trouble with my choruses.

SLICK: The rest of the piece ain't exactly platinum.

GLENNA RAE: Pay no mind, Bo. It's real nice. If Speed could have heard it, he would've been thankful.

CANDY: If Speed coulda heard it, Bo wouldn't a hadda sing it.

GLENNA RAE: *(Having heard enough from* CANDY...*)* Candy, I swear I could—

RICKY: Hey, what 'er we out here for? T'cry in our beer an bitch at one another?

TOAD: T'collect relics. From the wreck.

RICKY: Souvenirs.

TOAD: Ziggie calls 'em relics.

RICKY: Well, I came out here t'cut loose. Speed woulda wanted it. We're gonna party tonight.

BO PEEP: Yessiree, here we are in the ballroom of the Bellagio Hotel on the Las Vegas strip. *(To* CANDY *and* TOAD*)* You guys left the quarry too early.

TOAD: Too damn crowded.

CANDY: I was enjoyin' myself.

RICKY: But Ziggie wanted to leave so you two mutts went waggin' your tails behind.

(By now all are sharing a joint. They won't share with TOAD *until it's fairly exhausted. But when he's offered the roach he rejects it with, "I'm in trainin'." Then he spars a bit.)*

(There seems to be a sense of exhilaration that doesn't exist when ZIGGIE *is present.)*

BO PEEP: Sure see a lotta old faces on race weekend.

CANDY: Mostly ugly ones by my accountin'.

RICKY: They're all tryna relive old times at the quarry. Come Sunday, they truck their asses back t'their families an' their stupid lives.

CANDY: Some go back t'their stinkin' cities. An' their itty-bitty apartments.

SLICK: After tellin' us how good they're doin'.

RICKY: They go away, they should stay away. The quarry's ours now.

BO PEEP: Seen' Laura Jean Fletcher out there.

GLENNA RAE: Laura Jean. What a douche bag.

RICKY: Sonny Boy Brockett.

*(*TOAD *winds up and pitches an "air" baseball.)*

TOAD: Sonny Boy. Thought he'd play winter ball before his shot at the big leagues. Got slashed in his pitchin' arm in a Mexican whorehouse. *(Shaking his head and giggling)* What a loser.

BO PEEP: Charlene put 'er foot in 'er mouth out there.

GLENNA RAE: For *her* mouth, just another body part.

CANDY: *Charlene*??? Was she out there?

BO PEEP: *(Defensively)* Well…uh, yeah. She just stopped by.

CANDY: Did Ziggy… (?)

BO PEEP: She come over an' tried to move on him.

GLENNA RAE: He just looked right past her.

CANDY: *(Brightening)* Heyyyyy…that ain't easy considerin' alla room she takes up.

(They all laugh, more or less supportively.)

BO PEEP: Matter of fact, Zig said, "Fuck off, fatso."

CANDY: *(Elated)* He did? He said that? *(Mimicking)* "Fuck off, Fatso!"
That's real nice. Did she bring Rudy along?

GLENNA RAE: Oh…no. She said he was home in bed.

CANDY: Yeah, that raggedy-ass bastard can't keep up with "Charlene The Machine".
Hey Bo, what was it Charlene took up at college…big long word.

BO PEEP: Anthrypology.

CANDY: Yeah, that's diggin' up bones?

GLENNA RAE: Well, yeah. That's a start.

CANDY: This mornin' I said, "Where'd ya find Rudy, when you were bone diggin'?" Oh, she was pissed. She was always jealous of me since I was runner-up in the state beauty pageant. She still calls it a "contest", tryna get my goat. What would she know of pageantry?

BO PEEP: You woulda won, hon, iff'n you let me teach you the guitar.

CANDY: I figured my looks were enough. 'Sides, I mighta lost beauty points iff'n I cut my nails.

RICKY: You were doin' fine on *America The Beautiful* 'til you dropped the spoons.

(All laugh, including CANDY at what may be true.)

GLENNA RAE: Hey Slick, tell Candy how ya greeted Charlene.

TOAD: C'mon Slick, let's hear it.

SLICK: You can't hear it. You don't just conjure up a fart. She said, "Hey Slick The Sphinx; you still spend all day without a sound outta you?"

BO PEEP: That's when Slick let one fly.

SLICK: I'M TELLIN' IT!!!
She'd call me dummy back in school. So I sez, "I wasn't a dummy. I just never talked to *you*. That made me a smarty."

(SLICK *notices* TOAD's *sudden hurt.*)

SLICK: I didn't mean no harm, boy.

TOAD: Nah. A dummy is born mute. Momma just stopped talkin'. But I know she's thinkin' through her eyes. I take 'er dinner up every night an' she turns off the TV an' I tell 'er of my day. An she answers with blinks an' stares an' such. Told 'er about Speed tonight. I know that she'd pray for his soul an' his family. When you consider we were eleven kids they couldn't hardly feed…well, she coulda done worse than clam up. Lots worse. Lots have.

BO PEEP: (*After an awkward pause*) Charlene was askin' for you, Toad.

TOAD: G'wan. Charlene? For me?

BO PEEP: I said you were long gone by now. An' she said good, travelin's broadenin'.

RICKY: An Glenna says, "From the looks of yer ass, you been aroun' the world."

(*Laughter*)

BO PEEP: Maybe you shouldn'a said that. She consoled you on accounta Speed's tragedy.

GLENNA RAE: If it takes death to make her act decent, she can go piss up a rope.

RICKY: That crack she scored on me…I win a Purple Heart but she still brings up my record.

BO PEEP: You're not a real criminal, Rick. You were just afflicted with a severe case of joyridin'.

RICKY: Her daddy steals poor people blind. He got a whole lot fulla cars. I didn't figure he'd miss one. If I only I hadn't sold it…

TOAD: If you just returned it we wouldn'a had the greatest party in Provosnik's history.

(All agree heartily.)

CANDY: You shouldn'a blew all that dough at once.

BO PEEP: When you spend two grand in one weekend, the accusin' finger… *(She twirls her finger and points at RICKY.)*

TOAD: How was you t'know you were dancin' with a state trooper?

RICKY: She was too cute to be a cop. Hey, how many shrimp cocktails did you scarf down?

TOAD: Twenty-four.

GLENNA RAE: Then barfed 'em up in the parkin' lot. Acquired a taste and lost it all in one night. 'Member Ginger Kane threw the pool cue through the bar mirror?

TOAD: Ricky just handed Provosnik a coupla C-notes. You were cool, Rick.

GLENNA RAE: Poor Ginger. She was the best woman swimmer at the quarry.

BO PEEP: An' she died one night in the pool of the Miami Beach Ramada Inn.

TOAD: Who woulda known the pool had been drained? *(He mimes her fatal dive with his index and middle fingers)* Splat!

CANDY: I've been meanin' t'get down there. Do some personal investigation on my own. Ginger was too pretty to just die by accident.

BO PEEP: Samson Steele's conceited as ever. But he is a powerful hunk of young manhood...alla those muscles.

TOAD: He wasn't so powerful the night Ziggie cold-cocked 'im with one punch. Hadda sip his Ripple through a straw.

CANDY: *(Sneering)* Charlene always pushed Ziggie t'fight for 'er honor.

GLENNA RAE: A fight for Charlene's honor is a no-win contest.

BO PEEP: Like Toad at fight club.

TOAD: Someday...you'll see. Alla you will.

CANDY: Ziggie!

RICKY: I don't hear nothin'.

BO PEEP: Me neither.

CANDY: Ziggie for sure. I can hear his car ten miles off.

(The faint sound of a car [which becomes more intense]. The men grab the gear and start dismantling Speed's car. RICKY is disgruntled.)

(ZIGGIE's car pulls in with a screech. The stage is illuminated from his headlights. Then it goes dim.)

RICKY: Hey Zig, your lights would help considerably.

(ZIGGIE enters with a bottle. He is clearly stoned.)

TOAD: Hey Zig, are you smashed?

(ZIGGIE forcefully grabs terror-stricken TOAD. Indicating Speed's car...)

ZIGGIE: Given the circumstances, "smashed" is hardly a 'propriate word..

TOAD: *(Squirming)* Yeah, I shouldna said no such—

(Unpredictable ZIGGIE laughs and cuffs TOAD like a puppy. He hands TOAD what little is left of his bottle.)

TOAD: Thanks, Zig.

(A swig, then TOAD offers the bottle back to ZIGGIE who weighs the offer then thinks better of acceptance.)

ZIGGIE: It's O K. It's a present.

(TOAD is elated, more over the offer than the booze.)

RICKY: Hey, Zig?

ZIGGIE: Not makin' much progress.

RICKY: Hey, Zig!

ZIGGIE: Yo?

RICKY: *(Pointing off to ZIGGIE's car)* Lights.

ZIGGIE: Can't.

RICKY: Why can'tcha?

ZIGGIE: I beat you.

RICKY: What???

ZIGGIE: Up here.

RICKY: You left.

ZIGGIE: I came back.

RICKY: You forfeited.

ZIGGIE: I don't forfeit.

RICKY: What's this shit?

ZIGGIE: *Your* lights, Rick.

RICKY: *(Shaking his head)* What the—

ZIGGIE: High beams.

RICKY: Low beams.

ZIGGIE: I'll give us your high beams.

(ZIGGIE *starts off to* RICKY'*s car.* RICKY *intercepts him.*)

RICKY: No livin' man touches my car.

(*Tense moment then* RICKY *exits to his car. Momentarily, his high beams come on.*)

TOAD: (*Quietly*) Shrewd thinkin', Zig.

ZIGGIE: Simply a mutual misunderstandin' between gentlemen . I should think that fightin' friends is tougher than killin' A-rabs. .

(RICKY *re-enters.* ZIGGIE—*a changed man*—*throws his arm over* RICKY'*s shoulders.*)

ZIGGIE: Now, that wasn't so hard, was it ole buddy? (*Gesturing to the wreck*) You are the body and fender man. How about an expert's eye-view?

RICKY: (*Grumpily*) I charge for estimates.

ZIGGIE: (*Smiling as he shakes his head*) "I charge for estimates." The almighty dollar rears its ugly head. Whatcha workin' on?

RICKY: Gettin' me a door, here.

ZIGGIE: Atta boy, think big.
Toad?

TOAD: Workin' on this door handle ever since we arrived.

(*A couple of snickers from* BO PEEP *and* GLENNA)

ZIGGIE: Since you arrived, huh? Maybe you're doin' somethin' wrong.

TOAD: Gonna put it on my own buggy.

CANDY: What an obscenity.
My Uncle Luke had a new car for two days an' the handle came off in his hand.

(*Absolutely no reaction.* CANDY *shrugs, sips a beer.*)

ZIGGIE: See, this car's custom. Speed supervised. Read all about it in "Auto Freak Monthly". His team had pride. A vanishin' breed. Assembly line guys don't give a damn. Thass why our car industry is goin' belly-up.
Slick?

SLICK: *(Mumbles semi-coherently)* Fennrr.

ZIGGIE: "Fennrr", huh? You oughtta talk more, Slick. You're losin' your ability to communicate.

BO PEEP: You shoulda stayed in college after the broken leg.

SLICK: What for? There wasn't much there after sports.

GLENNA RAE: "What for"? An education, that's "what for".

SLICK: They recruited me for football, not education.

BO PEEP: God forbid you should learn somethin'.

SLICK: *(Waving a screw driver, threateningly)* Keep it up, Bo.

BO PEEP: Keep it up yourself. I'm not available. .

TOAD: *(Gleefully)* Hey, she got you there, buddy.

BO PEEP: Who's askin' you, pigshit? At least Slick doesn't move on my sheep.

(TOAD objects vehemently and all the others erupt except for ZIGGIE.)

ZIGGIE:Hey, hey, show some respect for the deceased.

CANDY: Just tryna pass the time, Zig.

ZIGGIE: Passin' time is your whole life.

CANDY: *(Coyly)* You know that ain't true.

ZIGGIE: Biggest hour of your day is in fronta the mirror every mornin'.

CANDY: I'm prouda my looks.

ZIGGIE:I'm ashamed of the rest of ya.

CANDY: *(Shaking her butt, cutely)* You ashamed of my *ass*ets?

ZIGGIE: You could at least show some concern for Sister Glenna Rae…drownin' in her sorras.

GLENNA RAE: Don't be so melodramatic. I'm drinkin' cause I like it.

ZIGGIE: You gotta get offa the hooch. You gonna wind up like your mother. Mrs D U I.

GLENNA RAE: Misdemeanors.

RICKY: Only cause she's local. When your momma's on a toot, I wish I was back in my tank.

ZIGGIE: You suffer real funny, Glenna.
Now let's get back to work.

RICKY: *(With a beam on Speed's car…and perhaps fabricating)* What about this engine, Zig? Smashed beyond repair. Even got bits an' pieces of flesh—

BO PEEP: DAMN!

ZIGGIE: *(Crossing)* A frightenin' sight, Rick.
Hey Glenna, come see what I'm so meladramatic about.
When that ole movie star got killed, James Dean…
when they dug him outta his Porsche the speedometer was buried in his belly. They pried 'er loose, an' it read one-thirty.

CANDY: *(Beat, and when that sinks in…)* Maybe it was the clock. Maybe he was killed at one-thirty.

(All look at CANDY and she shrugs.)

TOAD: I seen a pitcher of that Porsche somewheres… "Auto Freak Monthly"?

(The dog barks. ZIGGIE *takes some burger out of the cooler and starts off with crowbar in hand.)*

GLENNA RAE: *(In pursuit)* Ziggie! Don't! He's only a dog. Dogs bark!

ZIGGIE: It's only the junkman's half-dead pit bull. He's barkin' from pain.

GLENNA RAE: You a *vet*???

ZIGGIE: Ricky's the vet. An' this'll be an act of mercy.

BO PEEP: He's the grim reaper.

(He exits. GLENNA RAE *is frustrated...anguished...pained. Her fists and teeth are clenched.)*

BO PEEP: Don't let it get t'you, Gl—

GLENNA RAE: GET AWAY FROM ME!!! ALLA YOU!!! *(She crosses angrily, grabs her bottle and swigs.)*

RICKY: You should care for yourself like you care for that dog.

SLICK: *(Trying to focus elsewhere and referring to* TOAD*)* It wasn't *Auto Freak Monthly*.

TOAD: It wasn't?

(Conspiratorially, RICKY *and* SLICK *shake their heads.)*

TOAD: *Gear Box Gazette?*

*(*RICKY *and* SLICK *shake their heads.* TOAD *is perplexed.)*

TOAD: *NASCAR Review?*

RICKY: You seen it in *The Checkered Flag*.

TOAD: *(Confused) The Checkered Flag.* I dunno that one.

RICKY: You're not lookin' hard enough.

BO PEEP: Lotta valuable information.

RICKY: You're shortchangin' yourself, Toad.

CANDY: Missin' the boat..

SLICK: Droppin' the ball.

RICKY: Start gettin' *The Checkered Flag*.

TOAD: *(Befuddled, he nods)* Thanks, guys. I'll do that.

(An offstage "Yelp" is heard. Then another. Then a whimper. Then nothing. Everyone reacts, a couple of the women shudder. GLENNA RAE—a bit removed from the others—seems to wrap herself in a ball of pain. CANDY—in one of her few moments of enlightenment—opts to converse, albeit nervously.)

CANDY: I read somewheres that James Dean gave the first soul kiss in history.

BO PEEP: In *The Checkered Flag*?

RICKY: In history???

CANDY: Movie history.

BO PEEP: My momma had a thing for that James Dean. So I rented *East of Eden*. I've always been interested in Adam and Eve. Y'know, from Genesis. But they weren't in it and he showed me nothin'. Hell, when Otis Redding went down in that plane, now that was a true tragedy. Will Shakespeare could'na dreamed up a sadder one than that. Truly a loss t'music.

(ZIGGIE re-enters, commanding attention. The dog barks. ZIGGIE "yelps" —as he did offstage—to amusement and relief. TOAD imitates the yelp [poorly].)

GLENNA RAE: *(Half-laughing)* You son of a bitch, Zig. You sure had us—

ZIGGIE: You take me for a neanderthal, Glenna? Some beast? I love dogs more'n I do humans. How come *you* never thought t'feed 'er?

GLENNA RAE: *(Taken aback)* Well, no Zig…I knew you wouldn't have—

ZIGGIE: You're the washout, Glenna. Nobody expected much from us. But you had ambition...smarts. An' you waste your time with a buncha dead-enders.

(ZIGGIE *heads back to the project.* GLENNA RAE *stands with a bottle in hand. Since he has walked away she speaks in a vacuum...*)

GLENNA RAE: My ambition and my smarts are at opposite ends. (*Characteristically rebounding*) I knew you wouldn't hurt a pit bull, Ziggie. You're two of a kind.

ZIGGIE: (*Smiiling*) I'll take that as a compliment.

GLENNA RAE: (*Smiling back*) As intended.

(RICKY *gestures to* ZIGGIE *who steps forward and knocks the car door [or hood] loose with the crowbar.* ZIGGIE *lifts the piece in triumph.*)

ZIGGIE: Hang this over the door at Shorty's.

BO PEEP: If Shorty'll let you hang it there.

ZIGGIE: He'll let me hang it. (*Lowering the car part and indicating the tool box*) Hey Rick, pass over that ole box.

RICKY: (*Broad smile*) Hey Bo, you been paged.

BO PEEP: (*Angrily, she starts collecting her stuff to leave*) Fuck you, Roo Roo.

CANDY: Hey Bo, that rhymes.

GLENNA RAE: You're not talking t'your mother now, Ricky.

(SLICK *and* TOAD *hoot in derision of* RICKY.)

RICKY: You two are supposed t' be on my side.

TOAD: Not when yer getttin' whupped.

RICKY: (*To* GLENNA RAE) Keep my momma outta this. Just like *yours* has been kept outta every barroom in town.

(SLICK *and* TOAD *hoot in support of* RICKY).

BO PEEP: None a'the three of you have the brains to keel over if you were struck dead.

RICKY: We're talkin' kin, Bo? If your kid grows up an' has a child legit, she'll be breakin' with family tradition.

(BO PEEP *throws a beer can [or...?] at* RICKY.)

RICKY: (*Dodging the object and actually enjoying the conflict*) Ronette'll soon be peddlin' her tricycle to turn tricks at the quarry.

BO PEEP: Not for you, Dead-dick.

(*There is no hooting now, as* RICKY *is stung by the comment. He grabs the crowbar and* BO PEEP *scampers off. His bad leg makes his pursuit futile but grim-visaged* ZIGGIE *confrontationally intercepts him. Everyone tenses.* ZIGGIE *pushes* RICKY *once...twice...three times.* RICKY *raises the crowbar but* ZIGGIE *doesn't flinch. He lowers his head.*)

ZIGGIE: Go on. Go on, Rick. (*Not taunting, now, he's sincerely asking*) You have the guts to whack me, Ricky Roo Roo?

(*Everyone—including* BO PEEP *who has edged back on— focuses on* ZIGGIE's *bizarre behavior. Suddenly,* RICKY *howls and swings the crowbar amid screams. But he purposely hits the car [or the door or the hood].* RICKY *leaves the crowbar and walks away.* ZIGGIE *picks up the crowbar and follows him.*)

GLENNA RAE: Careful, Ziggie.

RICKY: (*Turning and facing* ZIGGIE) You gonna brain me?

(*Silently,* ZIGGIE *hands the crowbar to* RICKY.)

RICKY: Zig, I know you're flyin' high right now. An' somethin' bad happened out there today. Especially to you. But you're lucky you're facin' a man right now.

Samson Steele would love t'be in my shoes. He'd crush
your brains like Speed crushed his car.

(RICKY *drops the crowbar and turns away.* ZIGGIE *looks
around and after a deep breath...*)

ZIGGIE: Ladies and Gentlemen...it's prayer time. Let's
all gather around this here machine...what's left of 'er.
I'd like to express myself in a tribute...a kind of a—

BO PEEP: Eulogy?

ZIGGIE: Thank ya, Bo. A eulogy.

(*Only* CANDY *and* TOAD *really involve themselves.*
ZIGGIE *may stammer but he will invest his awkward speech
with passion. The others are more fascinated by* ZIGGIE's
preachment than by his "prayer".)

ZIGGIE: Lord, we place our hands on this once-proud
machine in tribute to it's once-proud driver, the late,
great and lamented, Hollis "Speed" Larsen, idol and
inspiration. He summoned up all the old virtues of
bravery, riches and faith in You, Lord to become a
genuine hero.

(*Skepticism by all but* CANDY *and* TOAD *[heading towards
euphoria] as* ZIGGIE *continues...*)

ZIGGIE: His flame flickered briefly on this earth but it
blazed like the devils own inferno.

(*The four exchange glances as he goes on...*)

ZIGGIE: Unlike other recent so-called martyrs in this
great land of ours, Speed was no seeker of self-interest
and propaganda. No siree, he was no elitist. He never
forgot he was a common man despite tasting caviar
and champagne and women.

(*This amuses* BO PEEP *especially, though she manages to
suppress a laugh as* ZIGGIE *concludes...*)

ZIGGIE: Yes, he made the small feel tall...

(Indicating the euphoric TOAD*)*

ZIGGIE: ...the country folk feel city. But most of all, Speed Larsen did what nobody else does anymore in this great land of ours...

TOAD: *(Eyes closed and shaking)* Whatzat, Zig? Whatzat? ...Whatzat?...

ZIGGIE: He kept our dreams alive.

CANDY: Amen, Zig. You said a mouthful.

TOAD: AMEN...AMEN...AMEN... *(He settles down.)*

BO PEEP: *(Half giggling)* Reverend Selby Baxter couldna said it no better.

GLENNA RAE: *(Drunk by now)* Bullshit!

ZIGGIE: You're wasted, Glenna. He shoulda meant somethin' t'you.

GLENNA RAE: He did. Somethin' long dead.

TOAD: *(Approaching peacefully)* Zig, our sister is just upset. The Lord forgives—

*(*ZIGGIE *kicks at* TOAD *and he skips away in retreat.)*

GLENNA RAE: Zig, *we* know the story out there, today.

ZIGGIE: What "story"?

GLENNA RAE: I hafta tell you?

ZIGGIE: Hey, the rest of you...take five.

(All head off slowly in the direction of ZIGGIE's *car.)*

ZIGGIE: Naw, naw, not that way. Other way.

(All head off elsewhere except for RICKY *who continues off towards* ZIGGIE's *car.)*

ZIGGIE: Hey Bo, play yer music. Play t'yer heart's content.

BO PEEP: Well gee, thanks Zig.

(Bo Peep hits the button on her C D player. The music fades as they go off.)

ZIGGIE: Now what're you babblin' about?

GLENNA RAE: You saw. You had the glasses. You saw how he stared at us.

ZIGGIE: He rekanized us.

GLENNA RAE: He had that look on his face. Said, "Death time, folks."

ZIGGIE: *(Flustered for a moment, then...)* Bullshit! He was happy. Rarin' t'go.

GLENNA RAE: Kept shakin' his head real slow.

ZIGGIE: That's...that's a nervous habit he got. Like a tic...when he's happy.

GLENNA RAE: *(A thumb down)* Then as he approached the start he gave us the "thumbs down".

ZIGGIE: *(Thumbs up, vehemently)* The high sign...high sign.

GLENNA RAE: Then he hit that startin' line, opened up that Golden Tiger Cat, went once around an' broke the all-time record. But he kept foot t'floor an' hit that concrete wall head-on.

ZIGGIE: Naw, naw, yer sufferin' from a fantasy causa what he meant t'ya. *(Shouting off)* BO! TURN THAT RACKET UP!

BO PEEP: *(Off)* Why Zig, I didn't know you were a music lover.

ZIGGIE: He crashed cause the streerin' column locked. Was onna news...was inna Sentinel.

GLENNA RAE: How d'you check that out in a mess like this? *(Indicating the car)* Zig, it wasn't a shameful thing. Speed was comin' apart...a man that lost the handle.

ZIGGIE: He was a champion. Champions don't go out that way.

GLENNA RAE: What're you, the resident authority on "champions"?

ZIGGIE: HEY BO, TURN THAT NOISE OFF AN' GET OUT HERE!

BO PEEP: *(As she turns the music off and re-enters)* Make up yer fuckin' mind. .

(SLICK and TOAD enter behind. RICKY enters from the opposite side, a big grin on his face.)

ZIGGIE: Seems there's a misunderstandin' about events, today. We all seen true an' clear, 'cept for Glenna. Her point of view is influenced by her...previous relationship with Speed.

RICKY: What's 'at "point of view", Zig?

ZIGGIE: Glenna says the accident was no accident. Thinks Speed had a death wish out there.

TOAD: *(Dumbfounded)* Su—icide? Cause he drove straight into the wall? Like Dale Earnhart?

RICKY: "Like *Dale Earnhart*"??? You little pissant. YOU CALLIN' DALE EARNHART A SUICIDE???

TOAD: *(Retreating defensively)* No, no, no, I'd never say any such thing, Rick.
I gotta go with you, Zig. Glenna's thinkin' carries no more weight than a cup fulla cotton.

ZIGGIE: Candy?

CANDY: Aw Zig, y'know I don't like decisions.

ZIGGIE: *(To GLENNA RAE)* Looks like twelve peepers seen what your two missed. We all viewed a mechanical failure.

SLICK: I think I'd like a say.

ZIGGIE: *(Ignoring this)* Well, sun's gonna be comin' up soon. Then back out t'the track.

GLENNA RAE: We goin' out there *again today???*

ZIGGIE: Today's race day. Gotta go,

GLENNA RAE: "Gotta go"? Who "gotta go"? I don't "gotta go"! Maybe you "gotta go". But I don't "gotta go".

TOAD: You don't wanna go?

ZIGGIE: Two reasons why we gotta go. When a tragedy occurs, you jump right back in. Gotta overcome the fear or you'll never return. Right, Rick?

RICKY: S'been my experience.

GLENNA RAE: If everyone stayed away then Speed would be alive today.

ZIGGIE: That ain't human nature. Secondly, Speed would want us t'go. It's the duty of a fan.

(In disgust, GLENNA RAE goes for her bottle.)

ZIGGIE: How 'bout the rest of you? Toad?

TOAD: I'm with you, Zig. Like always.

ZIGGIE: Atta boy. Candy?

CANDY: I'm aboard.

ZIGGIE: Right. We've been waitin' three hundred and sixty-four days for today. Now let's have a beer an' get back t'work.

(CANDY dutifully distributes beer. She tosses TOAD's at him and it foams when he opens it.)

SLICK: Hey Zig, I'd like a say.

ZIGGIE: Well, the Sphinx comes to life. You've earned a say as the finest running back this county has ever seen…thanks to my superior blockin'.

SLICK: *(Then he takes an inordinately long time to utter…)* I'm in.

ZIGGIE: Atta go, bro.

(ZIGGIE initiates a stylized "fist bump" between the two from their football days.)

(ZIGGIE's car horn sounds. All but RICKY and ZIGGIE are surprised. RICKY grins, having just seen ZIGGIE's car and its occupant. He addresses ZIGGIE…)

RICKY: Sleepin' Beauty's callin' Prince Charmin'.

GLENNA RAE: *(Drunkenly)* She been out there all this time?

BO PEEP: Not funny, Zig.

CANDY: *(Shouting off)* BLOW IT OUT YOUR ASS!!! Alla that education an' she's still a shitkicker. ZIGGIE'S PAYIN' HOMAGE T' SPEED. WHY DON'TCHA HAUL ASS? YOU DON'T BELONG HERE! *(She starts to pout quietly.)* Bitch ain't got an ounce a'pride. Think somebody who's been everywhere…seen everythin' would hate to come back t'this armpit town. *(To ZIGGIE)* When she an' that little weenie leave, they'll mock people like you… like me…like alla us. Just like always. They'll dis us in gas stations an' super markets…when we tend her garden an' collect her trash. Don't matter it's England. But when she's bitchin' about the service…I hope she recalls how far she flew for service from one of us.

ZIGGIE: She'll recall. An' you just hit on why I do it *to* her. Never *for* her.
So I gotta retreat briefly to the quarry.

CANDY: *(Clinging to him as she hollers off)* ZIGGIE'S SPOKEN FOR! ZIGGIE'S SPOKEN FOR!

(ZIGGIE wheels and slaps CANDY hard enough that she goes down.)

ZIGGIE: Nobody speaks for me!

TOAD: *(Rushing across)* No, not Candy, Zig. Candy's one a'us.

(ZIGGIE punches TOAD in the belly. He doubles up. RICKY chops him in the neck and TOAD goes down.)

(SLICK aggressively steps between TOAD and ZIGGIE. RICKY has backed away. SLICK and ZIGGIE lock eyes.)

RICKY: *(Fairly unhinged by now and referring to TOAD)* Why do we need this ball an' chain? Holdin' us back… draggin' us down. I'm sick of it.

ZIGGIE: *(Looking at TOAD)* He's got his good points.

(ZIGGIE uses this refocus on TOAD to back away from a dangerous confrontation with unflinching, intimidating SLICK.)

(The car horn sounds again.)

ZIGGIE: I'LL COME WHEN I'M READY!

CANDY: *(Quietly whimpering)* Can say that, again.

(CANDY and TOAD aren't really injured. It's happened before and will happen again.)

RICKY: Hey Zig, we're comin', too.

SLICK: Count me out! I'm walkin' home.

(Wanting no part of a confrontation, ZIGGIE just shrugs as SLICK continues aggressively…)

SLICK: See Zig, the fact is, I never liked you. I never even liked you on the field. I never liked you cause folks thought you were good when you were only dirty.

ZIGGIE: Sorry t'hear that Slick. But that's your choice. This here's America…a free country.

RICKY: C'mon, y'all. We're headin' for the quarry. Grab the gear.

Hey, Zig?

(ZIGGIE *turns to* RICKY *who points to the car door [or hood].* ZIGGIE *stares at the object.)*

RICKY: This here's the trophy. Speed's relic. Who gets it? You or me?

ZIGGIE: *(Pause, a gaze at the car part)* Fuck it!

(ZIGGIE *heads off as* RICKY *laughs in hysterical triumph. He then lifts the car part above his head.)*

RICKY: This is gonna look real good over my garage door.

GLENNA RAY: *(Drunkenly but sincerely to* CANDY*)* You O K, honey?

CANDY: In better shape than you. Not that you give a damn.

BO PEEP: We give a damn. It just doesn't matter. *(She starts off)*

CANDY: Then why are you leavin' with 'em?

BO PEEP: It's the only game in town.

CANDY: *(Shouting off at Charlene in* ZIGGIE's *car)* DON'T COUNT FOR MUCH WHEN YOUR COMPETITION'S A RICH SLUT!!!

(Charlene leans on ZIGGIE's *car horn, unrelentingly.)*

ZIGGIE: *(Off)* SHUT UP, CHARLENE1 JUST GET OFFA THAT HORN!!!

(The car horn stops.)

(GLENNA RAE— *sitting on an old car seat or a hood* — *laughs at* ZIGGIE's *comment. She's attached to a bottle of her own.)*

(Still on the ground, CANDY *can smile at* ZIGGIE's *trashing of Charlene.)*

ZIGGIE: *(Off)* SEE YOU HALF WITS LATER!

(ZIGGIE *howls the last laugh, turns on his ignition and pulls away with a screech. It's nearly sun up as indicated by the stage lighting.*)

(SLICK *goes to* RICKY's *cooler, opens it and takes a beer. Offended* RICKY *looks at* SLICK *who opens the can and places the beer next to the recovering* TOAD. SLICK *tousles* TOAD's *hair.* RICKY *knows better than to object about the confiscated beer.*)

RICKY: You ain't comin' t'the quarry, Slick?

SLICK: Naw. Like I said, I'm walkin'. I need t'get back in shape. I'm headin' out on Monday.

RICKY: You plannin' a comeback? I hear you been eyein' Canadian football.

SLICK: *(Shaking his head)* I'm headin' t'The Middle East.

(RICKY *is practically pole-axed. He's feverish in his reaction. The others pop to attention.*)

RICKY: You're goin'…t' THE MIDDLE EAST??? Are you fuckin' crazy? You bought that recruitment bullshit? You gonna risk your life for a bunch of fat-cat oilmen…crooked contractors? For towelheads who want you dead. You're cannon fodder, Slick!

SLICK: You got it all wrong, Rick.

RICKY: I got it wrong??? I was there, Slick. I'm the one who can't get treatment at the vet's hospital. Can't get a decent job with my leg. An' you're telling me that—

SLICK: I ain't goin' as military. I'm guardin' those fat cat mothafuckers.

RICKY: You're a fuckin' *mercenary*???

SLICK: Uh…they tell me I'm "security". Nine hundred bucks a day. Up to fifteen hundred after a year.

BO PEEP: Hey, big bro Slick. Had enough of these pale-ass honkies? Let's you an' me--

RICKY: How'd you manage—

SLICK: My ole college coach. He recruits studs for Blackwater. *(Smiling broadly)* "See Momma, college *did* pay off. "

RICKY: *(Pathetically…sadly…howling and on the verge of tears)* OOOOOHHHHHHhhhhh, Goddddd. I get my… balls shot off…my life in…the toilet for a pack of lies. Why…why me? Why wasn't I a mercenary???

SLICK: *(Not smart-assedly but matter-of-factly)* Well Rick, I guess I'm just a badder mothafucker than you.

(RICKY pulls himself together and heads off with BO PEEP. She helps with the car door and the cooler. As he's about to exit he turns to SLICK.)

RICKY: Good luck, man. Watch yer ass over there.

SLICK: Yeah. I'm gettin' me a steel-plated jock strap.

(RICKY shakes his head and he and BO PEEP exit. GLENNA RAE is passed out and basically unnoticed.)

BO PEEP: *(Off)* You guys comin'?

(CANDY and TOAD shake their heads.)

SLICK: *(To CANDY and TOAD)* See you guys.

TOAD: Good luck, dude.

CANDY: Be careful, man. We love ya.

(SLICK exits opposite BO PEEP and RICKY just as we hear RICKY's car grinding from a dead battery.)

RICKY: *(Off)* SONOFABITCH, ZIGGIE!!! Come on, Bo. Let's walk it,

(We hear two car doors slam.)

CANDY: *(Calling off)* You may be a body an' fender man, Rick. But you sure don't know batteries.

(A beer can comes flying on and CANDY laughs as she avoids it.)

CANDY: How you doin', boy?

TOAD: Oh, I'm O K. Betcha I piss blood, though.

CANDY: That's the wound you suffered for comin' t'my defense.

TOAD: I'll piss my wound away. If I hadda scar it would remind me of you.

CANDY: *(An odd look)* You need a scar to think of me?

TOAD: Poor Ricky. You think Bo can help him any?

CANDY: Not if the doctor's can't. What can Bo do? She told me she could love Ricky, y'know? But a girl needs a man with a bone.

(TOAD shakes his head and CANDY helps him up. They are oblivious to GLENNA RAE [herself oblivious].)

TOAD: Hey if you went with them it'd just be more booze an' dope all day an' then facin' ole Wilcox on Monday.

CANDY: Maybe I walk out on Wilcox. Maybe I quit this town. Right now!

TOAD: Well, Ziggie's hard on you but I betcha he's worse on her.

CANDY: But she likes it. I don't.

TOAD: He'll be on your cell callin' you tomorra.

CANDY: That's not enough t'make me wanna stay.

TOAD: How would you get out? No busses on Sunday.

(CANDY strikes a hitchhiking pose, her rear angled. TOAD mimes a wide-eyed driver and verbally screeches.)

TOAD: *(A sweeping bow)* Climb aboard my chariot, my pretty princess.

CANDY: Well, thank you my handsome Prince of The Turnpike.

(CANDY and TOAD giggle like kids.)

CANDY: I could make it t'some big city. Get a job dancin'…show business…modelin'. Somethin' like that. Then I'd come back in a coupla years loaded down with finery. Stuff earned. Not *given'* t'me by my daddy.

TOAD: Not even yer "sugar daddy"?

CANDY: Maybe a sapphire or two. I won't chase after Zig though. I'll 'knowledge him. I'll 'knowledge alla you. But y'all will be doin' the same things. I mean, you…you talk about Switzerland an'—

TOAD: Sweden. But that was Delmer's dream. I got it good, here. I can retire in twenty-four years with a pension.

CANDY: That's for sure. There's always gonna be garbage.

TOAD: It's easy for you t'leave. You make friends real easy. But me…it was a lesson I just been taught.

CANDY: So, you wouldn't defend me again?

TOAD: I would. Defendin' you is like instink.

CANDY: *(Smiles, shakes her head)* Well, I'm splittin'. You wouldn't have a mirror?

TOAD: Don't use one.

(CANDY gives a little wave as she heads off.)

TOAD: Hey, yer goin' the wrong way. 265 is north.

CANDY: You dumb peckerwood. Y'think I'm leavin' with the clothes on my back?
Besides, I needa think about it.

(TOAD reaches into his pocket, extracts his "silver ball" and holds it out to CANDY in the palm of his hand.)

CANDY: You tryna be funny? Get away from me with that trashball.

(CANDY *whacks it out of* TOAD'*s hand. He watches until it comes to rest. Then like an obedient pup, he "fetches" and addresses retreating* CANDY.)

TOAD: It's all I have for your goin' away.

CANDY: *(Stops, turns...)* Well, what about...I thought you were savin' it up for the war.

TOAD: I'd rather give it to someone beautiful than for something' terrible.

CANDY: *(Genuinely)* You're a real romantic guy, Toad.

TOAD: Yeah. *(Stammers)* I always...always...always...

CANDY: I know. *(Touching him gently)* I've always known.

TOAD: Then why are you always so mean t'me?

CANDY: I dunno. I never...well...I just don't wanna... encourage you.

TOAD: *(Nods...reflects a moment...)* Yeah. I wouldn'a encouraged me.

(CANDY *kisses* TOAD *gently on the cheek. They separate.*)

TOAD: Well...see ya, *Florinda.*

CANDY: Lord, you know how much I hate that name... *Carlton.*

(CANDY *and* TOAD *smile. She turns and exits.*)

(*Early morning sounds. He watches her then turns, kicks a beer can then notices* GLENNA RAE).

TOAD: I didn't know you was still here, Glenna. You gonna be aright? Need some help?

(*No response from the unconscious* GLENNA RAE. *She still has her bottle in hand.*)

TOAD: S'arright. You always make it home. Dream one for me.

(TOAD *takes off his shirt and positions it so that* GLENNA *is shielded from the sun. Then he heads off opposite of* CANDY *[and on the trail of* BO PEEP *and* RICKY*]. Suddenly he stops and returns to Speed's wreck. He picks up a door handle. He wipes it on his shirt, huffs on it and buffs it again. Satisfied, he sticks it in his pocket. But he looks to* GLENNA RAE *with concern. Worriedly, he approaches her and drops to his knees in front of her. He bends down and tries to listen for a heartbeat.)*

GLENNA RAE: Don't touch the titties!

(Semi-alarmed by GLENNA RAE, TOAD *vehemently shakes his head in embarrassment. He rises and looks skyward. She is passive again so he utters to himself…*

TOAD: Gonna be hot as a bitch t'day. *(He hustles off calling…)* HEY, WAIT FOR ME.

(The bottle rolls out of GLENNA RAE's *hand as the lights dim.)*

END OF PLAY